CARLO DEGLI ESPOSTI - GIANCA
ORIANO TASSINARI CLÒ - FAB

BOLOGNA

alma mater studiorum

Published by
ITALCARDS
bologna Italy

Sole distributor for Bologna and its province
Via S. Pio V, 19/A - ☎ 550487 - 40131 BOLOGNA

Second revised edition
Revisions by Oriano Tassinari Clò

Graphics and typesetting by:
Federico Frassinetti

Photographs by: Ascanio Ascani / Forlì

Other photographs by: CNB & C. - Cabicar - Publi Aer Foto /
Milan - Gnani Brother - Federico Frassinetti - Bruno Marino -
Ezio Quiresi / Cremona - Mario Rebeschini - Studio Image Line

editions **ITALCARDS** bologna - italy
© Copyright **1993** La Fotometalgrafica Emiliana Spa

---

*In the previous page: the «Sigillum magnum Studii
generalis bononiensis», designed by Augusto Sezanne for
the University's eighth centenary (1888). It sports the
famous motto LEGUM BONONIA MATER - PETRUS
UBIQUE PATER, the cross and the town's bearings.
The Gothic-styled polyptych includes also sacred images:
the Madonna with Child and St. Catherine of Alexandria
(coat-of-arms of «Universitas Iuristarum»); Saints Cosma
and Damiano («Universitas Artistarum»); the Madonna
with Child and four kneeling Doctors («Collegium
Iuridicum Pontificium»); St. Luke the Evangelist
(«Collegium Medicum et artisticum»); the Annunciation
(«Collegium Iuridicum Civilis»).*

2

Location and Urban Development

Bologna is the pole of Italy's communication system because of its location between the continental and the peninsular parts of the country; it is therefore the main link between North and South, the Tyrrhenian and Adriatic coasts through its road, railroad and also airway systems. Bologna's railway junction is one of the most important in the country while the Bologna-S. Donato freight depot, located East of the town is one of the largest in Europe.

Bologna is not only the main economic and cultural centre of the Emilia-Romagna Region but also its administrative capital, which can be easily reached from all the towns of Emilia and Romagna thanks to its central location.

The town lies at the foot of the Appennines' mountain range which encircles it from the South with its verdant and pleasant wooded hills dotted with villas, parks and old monasteries. From their tops the eye can spatiate on the city, the Po valley down to the Alps' foothills and the Euganean hills. In the other directions lies a fertile plain which is rationally and intensively cultivated and dotted with active rural centres. The town's expansion is mostly concentrated towards the North (Bolognina and Corticella) and in the East-West directions along the Emilian Way which is one of the main arteries in the Region. New settlements have sprouted, thus enlarging the city at whose fringes lie many high-tech and specialized small and medium size industries, shopping centres and wholesale distribution centres. On the contrary, the hillsides have kept intact their scenic beauty of great impact beside forming a sort of green belt vital to the town and its inhabitants.

---

1. Towers and steeples dot the skyline of Bologna.

The old town's centre is one of the best preserved throughout Europe and in Italy it is second only to Venice. Its boundaries are marked by a ring of tree-lined avenues following the layout of the lastly-built ancient walls a few traces of which still remain, besides ten out of the twelve gateways giving admittance to the town in ancient times.

The old urban centre deriving from the original Roman plan (of which many remains have resurfaced) kept on expanding from the 11th century onwards — after a period of reversed trend during the High Middle Ages — following a circular plan. The main roads are placed radially and converge on the main junction points which correspond to the poles of the Emilian Way within the town's boundaries: Malpighi's square to the West and the square of Ravegnana Gate, where the Two Towers stand, to the East.

The urban layout is characterized by long rows of arcades, varying in size and forms, which are one of the peculiar aspects of the town and create fantastic light and shade lacings and spectacular perspective views. With its rows of arcades, 35 km long, from the wooden ones belonging to Medieval houses to the severe and pointed archways of the 14th-15th centuries, from the spatious ones of the Renaissance and the Baroque periods to the humble and narrow ones of the poor quarters, Bologna has to offer a fascinating gallery of architectural examples unique in its genre and therefore can be justifiably called one of the world's most scenic town.

Another characteristic of the town is the warm-toned quality of the terracotta tiles and brickworks of the houses' faces which give Bologna its peculiarly unique and evocative red-ocre colouring.

1. The 15th century Drapers' Palace. 2. Tomb of Odofredo and a partial view of the apse and the belfries of S. Francis. 3. A daring «upside down» effect: the Asinelli Tower behind the basilica of S. Bartolomeo. 4. Piazza Maggiore from the Arengo Towen.

4

The town centre, which in part has already being turned into pedestrian malls or in which circulation of private vehicles is restricted, hosts main institutional and administrative buildings, the major cultural and learning centres (the University, museums, libraries, etc.), the great palaces of the noble families and the most important places of worship. The remains of Medieval towers and turrets, not a few in number, look down on those buildings from their height. These towers justify the appellation of *la turrita* (city of towers) given to Bologna. This area is surrounded by a varied network of streets and buildings of great urbanistic interest even in its more modest aspects, whose conservation has been made possible thanks also to a plan of environmental and social improvement aimed at the restoration of characteristic popular housing quarters (S. Leonardo, Miramonte, S. Carlo, S. Caterina).

In more recent years, the area to the North of the town was chosen, according to a rationally laid-out plan for the decentralization of services, as suitable ground for the building of important cultural and economic structures (Permanent Fair Grounds, Business Centre and the Stock Market Centre, the Palace for Cultural activities and Conferences, the Town's Modern Art Gallery, the Region's Administrative headquarters, the main offices of Banca del Monte di Bologna e Ravenna, of SIP (National Communication and Telephone Company) and RAI (National Television Station). These buildings together with the *Fiera District* and its staggering towers designed by Architect Kenzo Tange are the poles of attraction around which the modern part of Bologna rotates. Other structures, as the Slaughterhouse, the Livestock Market, the Entrepot and the Wholesale Commercial Centre (Centergross). have also been decentralized while efficient community centres open to the public have been established in suburban areas.

Brief History of the Town

Thanks to its location at the fringes of the Appennines and by lying at a sort of dividing line between the Northern, central and Southern parts of Italy, Bologna with its rich and fertile soil has been since the 9th century B.C. the area of settlement for peoples engaged in agriculture, animal breeding and already mastering the art of bronze casting, as we can see in the rich troves found in surrounding areas, especially Villanova of Castenaso, site from which the Villanovan

1. The «heart» of the town's centre between the churches of St. Peter and St. Petronius. Radiating streets spread out to the east, beyond the Two Towers.

culture has derived its name.

Dating back to the second half of the 6th century B.C., the town of *Felsina* founded by the Etruscans and called *princeps Etruriae* in the old days soon became a very important centre of trade thanks also to its strategic location. It had its own sanctuary on a hilltop close to the settlement with a necropolis around it. In the 4th century B.C. the town was run over by the Gallic tribes of the Boi who settled there. The new name of *Bononia* given to the town, from the Celtic word *bona* = building (at least according to some experts), and kept also by the Romans after their conquest in 191 B.C., perhaps for its well-wishing sounding quality, has been ascribed to them. Two years later three thousand families of Latin colonists headed by Senators Lucius Valerius Flaccus, Marcus Attilius Serano and Lucius Valerius Tappone settled in the territory. With the opening of the Emilian Way (187 B.C.) Bononia became one of the poles of the Roman road system; through the *Minor Flaminian Way* it was linked to Arezzo and through the *Altinate Emilian Way* to Aquileia.

In 88 B.C., when it was given the status of Municipality, the town had a quadrilateral plan with a street layout formed by six cardi and eight decumani still in existence today. It was also provided with a well-run sewer system and an aqueduct which provided the town with the water taken from the Appennines, at a distance of twenty km.

During the Roman Ages *Bononia* had a population of about 20.000 people, temples and majestic public buildings, such as baths, a theatre (of which in 1982 important remains were brought to light in Carbonesi street), and almost certainly an arena near today's Church dedicated to the Saints Vitale and Agricola. «*Culta Bononia*», as Martial calle it

in one of his epigrams, was a meeting point for different civilizations; in the 1st century A.D. Pomponius Mela placed it among the five «most opulent» Italian towns. During the reign of the Emperor Claudius it was greatly ravaged by a fire but was rebuilt with new and grander public buildings under Nero who favoured it greatly.

After a long period of decadence (St. Ambrose called it at the end of the 4th century A.D. a «corpse-like town in shambles»), the town's flourishing started in the 5th Century at the time

---

1. The wooden arcade (13th century) of Palazzo Grassi. 2. The 16th century arcade of Poggi Palace. 3. Malvezzi Campeggi Palace seen from the arcade of S. Giacomo church (15th century). 4. The Arengo Tower rises above the King Enzo and Podestà palaces. 5. The «red-hued» town framed by verdant rolling hills.

of Bishop Petronius, who became later on the Patron Saint of Bologna and to whom many public buildings and the creation of St. Stephen's church complex, inspired by the places of worship related to Christ's Passion in Jerusalem, are allegedly ascribed. The town, which was a sort of bridge-head for the Byzantines, placed as it was at the Western fringes of the Ravenna Esarcate, was enclosed by walls following a square layout which left outside most of the earlier Roman settlement already in ruins (*civitas antiqua rupta*). In 728 it was conquered by Liutprando, thus becoming part of the Langobard Kingdom. At the time of this annexation to the Langobard kingdom, St. Stephen's group of churches became one of the main Italian places of worship of the High Middle Ages — even Charlemagne stopped there in 786 — not only for its symbolic value but also for the relics of the protomartyrs Vitale and Agricola from Bologna which were kept there.

In the 11th century Bologna, which kept on expanding demografically as well as economically, was one of the first cities to assume the status of free-township: in 1164 it joined the Lombard League against Emperor Frederick Barbarossa. At the same time, the *Studium*, the oldest European University (by tradition the year of foundation is thought to be 1088), was flourishing. Many famous masters at Law (the so-called «glossatori») such as Irnerius, Bulgarus, Martinus, Rolandino de' Romanzi, Ugo, Iacopo, Azzo and Accursius contributed to spread its fame throughout Europe and gathered around them large groups of young students from all over the continent. These students were called, according to their country of origin, Citramontani (that is from this side of the Alps: Lombards, Tuscans and Romans) and Ultramontani (from countries

lying beyond the Alps: French, Spanish, English, Burgudians, Normans, Catalans, Hungarians, Polish, Germans, and also from Piccardy, Turennes, Poitou, etc). Dante, Petrarca and Boccaccio were also students of the University.

In the meanwhile and since the 12th century, Bologna had seen to it to protect itself by erecting new walls, commonly known as the walls of the year «one Thousand» or of the «Torresotti», in order to respond to the town's expansion.

---

1. The Gothic portal of the Merchants' palace with the screen by Rubbiani. 2. Bolognini Palace (15th century) near St. Stephen's church. 3. Ancient buildings seen from the Merchants' Loggia. 4. Via D'Azeglio towards the Clock Tower.

In the second half of the 13th century a third larger series of walls was erected, corresponding to today's tree-lined avenues encircling the city. These walls, which were completed only during the following century, had become necessary so as to include within the town the new urban settlements lying already outside the second older walls.

The 13th century marks the period of higher splendour and greater political, military and economic power for Bologna which rested not only on the fame of the Studium as a pole of attraction but also on the highly significant victory over the Imperial forces in the battle of Fossalta in 1249. King Enzo, the son of Emperor Frederick II, was captured in the battlefield, brought to Bologna and kept in a palace, which was later named after him, as a prisoner under a benevolent but inflexible watch till his death (1272), despite the threats and appeasements of his father to set him free. The 13th century represents also the epoch of great social and economic reforms. Among these, the «Law of Paradise» stands out for its fundamental importance because through this 1256 Act Bologna, the first in Europe, abolished serfdom by buying off the serfs with public money and employing them in farming activities which were in need of labour to respond to the current economic boom. This development had been brought about by the great numbers of foreign students coming to town and by the consequent inflow of wealth which contributed to create new opportunities for trade and exchanges, to set up new activities and to spur farmers to grow more food and make available on the market larger stocks of produce.

It was in that period that Bologna became to be called with the nick-names of *la grassa* (fat city) as well as *la dotta* (learned city), still in use

1. Archiginnasio: the austere courtyard (16th century). 2. Bevilacqua Palace (15th century) with its lovely courtyard. 3. Corbelling and open galleries in the courtyard of Ghisilardi Fava Palace (15th century). 4. The grand staircase of the Prefect's Caprara Palace.

today. Meanwhile the town had seen its sky-line transformed by the raising of many towers and turreted houses which soon became its main feature (today only the remains of forty of them are still visible). Grand public buildings and imposing monasteries and cloisters such as the ones built for the new Mendicant Orders of St. Dominic and St. Francis were also erected. Therefore Bologna could be listed among the ten most populated cities of Europe in 1294.

A short period of political and economic decline was the consequence of violent internecine struggles that in 1274 resulted in the expulsion of the Lambertazzi's Ghibelline faction and in scorching military defeats such as the one at Zappolino in 1325 at the hands of the Modenese. This decline reached its peak in the third decade of the 14th century when the town fell definitively under the influence of the Church with far-reaching consequences because in practice, if not in name, it deprived Bologna of its full sovereignity (in fact the town reaffirmed always its independence and considered itself bound only by an alliance with the Pope). After the happy but short-lived period during which Taddeo Pepoli ruled the town (1337-47), the Visconti family held it under their yoke until 1360 when it fell again under the Pope's rule, thanks also to the strong political and military action of Card. Egidio Albornoz.

In time the town was to fall alternatively under the rule of the Visconti family and the Pope with brief interludes of autonomous and republican government (such as the one of the «Free-State Reformers», established in 1377 and during which marvelous buildings such as St. Petronius's Church and the Merchants' Loggia were initiated). As for the town's most important families, they continued to vie with each

others for supremacy. Finally, around 1450, the Bentivoglio family gained the upper hand, and the rule, first with Sante (1445-62) and then with Giovanni II (1462-1506) who strengthened their hold on the town. During the Bentivoglio's rule, Bologna underwent not only an exceptional ur-

1. *Tomb of Rolandino de' Romanzi near St. Francis' church.*
2. *Tomb of Rolandino de' Passeggeri near St. Dominic's church.* 3. *Detail of the marble ark of Giovanni da Legnano.*
4. *Detail of the ark of Bonifacio Galluzzi.*

ban renewal and saw an extraordinary flourishing of new works of art but also became a lively cultural centre with two poles, the University and the intellectual circles at the court of Giovanni II. The refreshing and uplifting Renaissance spirit within the sombre walls of Bologna changed its whole outlook: houses and whole quarters were changed; while new churches and palaces were built, old ones were renovated and embellished with precious new artworks. Internecine strifes and far-reaching political reasons, as the Pope's intolerance for the Bentivoglio's growing power, set the down-fall of Giovanni II in 1506. The town was sieged by the Pope Julius II and his army, Giovanni was forced to leave and his palace, one of the most beautiful noble abodes in Italy at that time, razed to the ground and all its works of art pillaged by the townfolks.

From the expulsion of the Bentivoglio to the end of the 18th century, Bologna remained under the strong rule of the Pope for almost three centuries. It was part of the Papal States and ruled by a government formed by a Legate Cardinal representing the Pope and the town's Senate which elected the Gonfaloniere of justice aided by eight elder Consuls every two months. During that long rule, the town enjoyed a long period of peace and economic stability, without any great jolts except for the famine at the end of the 16th century, when the population fell from 72,000 to 59,000, or the famous plague of 1630 that reduced it to 47,000 (a few decades after the plague the population was to grow up to 60-65,000, level that was to remain stable up to the end of the 18th century).

During the 16th century, Bologna played an important role on the international scene: in 1515 Pope Leo X met there Francis I, King of France;

1. The Specola Tower (18th century) looks down on the University compound. 2. Ancient instruments in the Astronomy Museum. 3. The Hercules by Angelo Piò in Poggi Palace. 4. The Banner (1888) of the «Alma Mater Studiorum».

Charles V was crowned Emperor of the Holy Roman Empire by Clement VII (in 1530 the Pope was to call under the shadow of the Two Towers the political leaders of Italy and Europe of that time); after the transfer in 1547 of the Council from Trent to Bologna, several sessions were held there; the Pope Paul III visited the town in 1543 and Pope Clement VIII in 1572 and on both occasions huge public celebrations were organized (as was the case for the election in 1572 of the Bolognese Ugo Boncompagni as Pope Gregory XIII). Major urban renewal works changed little by little the whole outlook of the town: in 1564 the square of the Neptune was opened up, while the Archiginnasio, destined to house permanently the seat of the University, and the front of the Banchi Palace, thus completing the ring of buildings facing Piazza Maggiore (the Main Square), were erected almost at the same time. New imposing places of worship crowned with their beauty the town centre thanks not only to the settlement in Bologna of new religious orders (Jesuits, Barnabites, Fathers of the Oratorians, Fatebenefratelli, etc.) but also to the enlargement and restructuring of the old churches and monasteries (St. Michael in the Woods', St. Salvatore's, St. John on the Mount's, St. Dominic's, St. Mary of the Serfs', etc.). With its 96 big monasteries Bologna held the first place in Italy, as it was also recalled by foreign travellers in the 18th century. At the same time many imposing palaces, built by Senators' families, were erected: often without the traditional arcades and most of them enlivened by rich and elaborate Ba-

roque staircases and precious paintings. The inside decorations were made by local masters of the flourishing painting school of Bologna which soon became famous throughout Europe, thanks to its most outstanding members such as the Carracci brothers, Reni, Albani, Guercino, Domenichino, Franceschini, the Bibiena family and Giuseppe Maria Crespi. Between the 16th and 18th centuries Bologna was to gain its characteristically unique scenic outlook which is still today its main feature.

At the beginning of 18th century Bologna appeared to have attained a certain degree of wealth thanks to farming, the hemp and silk textile industries as well as meat packing (the famous Bologna sausages) and other activities. Let us recall also the new Institute of the Sciences founded in 1711 by General Luigi Ferdinando Marsigli, which came to be placed, in order of importance, alongside the older University — out of which famous masters such as Aldrovandi, Malpighi, and Galvani still came — and which soon became one of the most important and active European research centres. Then, magnificent public and private parties and celebrations were held especially when famous people were

---

1. Archiginnasio: the upper open gallery. 2. Irnerius by Luigi Serra in the Municipal Palace. 3. The arcades of St. Luke and the Charterhouse lying in the town's outskirts.

passing through the town which was already somewhat satisfied of its role of Northern provincial capital of the Papal States while the real power was firmly in the hands of the Senatorial oligarchy. With the fulmineous power-taking by Napoleon Bologna was to live through a real upheaval: at first it became the capital of the Cispadane Republic and later on the second centre of the Cisalpine Republic and the Kingdom of Italy after Milan, thereby becoming an extremely active pole of the cultural, political and economic life.

In the 45 years following the Restauration of the Pope's rule the town was the arena of several uprisings, especially the ones of 1831 and 1848 which culminated, on 8th August 1848, in the throwing out of the Austrian oppressors in the struggle for independence. After the visit of Pope Pius IX in 1857, on 12th June 1859 Bologna voted its annexation to Piedmont and became part of the united Kingdom of Italy. Therefore, its position as Italy's vital communication link was enhanced and the fame of its old University took on a fresh start thanks also to the activity of famous masters and teachers such as Carducci, Pascoli, Righi, etc.. In 1888 solemn celebrations for the 800th anniversary of the University's foundation were held with the participation of the King, Umberto I, and representatives of all the Universities of the world.

At the same time the town was growing beyond the boundaries of its walls which were finally pulled down at the beginning of the 20th century as new and thriving industrial and commercial activities were established. Between the end of the 19th century and the first three decades of the 20th, new streets were opened up by razing buildings and therefore the old layout of the town centre was modified without loosing, however, its unique architectural harmony which was later given the priority in the urban renewal plans carried out by the Municipality from the 1960's.

During World War II, the town was heavily bombed and damaged (we should also recall here the heavy toll in human lives paid by Bologna during the Liberation struggle, for which it was honoured by a gold medal, the second one in its history, to be pinned on the town's flag) but the war's open wounds were soon healed. From 1945 to the present day, Bologna has seen the continuous growth of its economy thanks to its numerous highly-specialized small and medium-size industries, its thriving service activities and its trade and distribution centres, which have sprung up also owing to the creation of the expressway link-up and the opening of the Guglielmo Marconi Airport. In more recent years, in the town's northern suburbs the new *Fiera District*, designed by the Japanese architect Kenzo Tange, was built.

It comprises not only the permanent fair grounds but also the Municipal Modern Art Gallery, the modern Palace for Culture and Conferences, the Business Centre, the Commodity Exchange Market, the main offices of the Region, of R.A.I, S.I.P., of Banca del Monte, and the tall towers, housing offices and services, which have already become the symbols of a town looking towards the future.

«Guinness book's» records

Among the many attributions given to Bologna the most common is the one of *turrita* (city of towers). They may not certainly have been 200 or even 180, as is allegedly believed (and as many guidebooks still report) but the towers dotting the skyline of Bologna within its walls in the 12th and 13th centuries were really many. We can still see the remains of about forty towers, some of which are practically intact, as the Asinelli (m.98) and Garisenda (m.48) towers, now the symbols of the town, the Incoronata (m.59) and Altabella (m.60) ones, standing high and agile, the Galluzzi (m.32), Uguzzoni (m.60), towering over meandering Medieval streets on Mandria alleyway, the

Passipoveri and Scappi ones. Others, instead, have lost their tops or have fallen in ruins over the centuries and their sad remains have either been included in old palaces or turned into roof-terraces or steeples as was the case for the towers Alberici, Agresti, Catalani, Guidozagni, Ghisilieri, Oseletti, Prendiparte, Dalle Perle, Carrari, Caccianemici, and others more. Besides being a record number, these towers surely make of Bologna a unique town full of enchanting fascination.

Another record is set by the endless and scenic rows of arcades that meander along the streets in a fantastic game of light and shade and perspective illusions, thus giving origin to another unique architectonic characteristic of the town. All the arcades have their special intimate beauty: from the wooden ones of Medieval houses to the severe porches of the 14th-15th centuries or from the harmonious ones of the Renaissance to the Baroque ones, form the arcades of noble palaces and big churches to the narrow ones of humble abodes. Bologna is the town with the highest number of arcades in the world: they are 35 km long and offer an unmatched architectonic view. Also — here again another record setting — Bologna has the longest known arcade: it is the one linking the town to the St. Luke Sanctuary on the Della Guardia hill. Dating back to the 17th century, it is longer than 3 km and for the most

part climbs along the steep side of the hill. It is also possible to reach the Sanctuary of the St. Luke's Madonna through a continuous covered «gallery» (except for the street crossings) 8 km long starting from the Alemanni Church outside Porta Maggiore (Main Gate) on the eastern part of town.

Finally, another curious characteristic: the Archiginnasio Palace, built in 1563 as the permanent seat of the ancient Bologna University, has more than 7,000 coats of arms of Italian and foreign students that from the 16th to the 18th centuries held honorary posts in the University: painted in bright colours on the walls and vaults of open galleries, staircases, hallways and rooms, they represent a unique heraldic collection which makes Bologna to stand out for another peculiar record.

1. Winter scenes: in Neptune's square... 2. ...at the Two Towers... 3. ...and in the Merchants' square. Page 22 and 23. Beautiful Piazza Maggiore, the pulsing heart of the town's artistic and civic life.

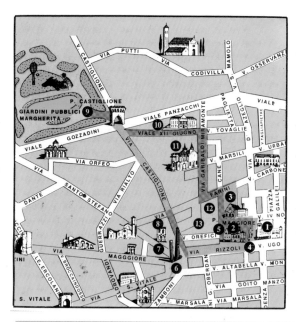

Piazza Maggiore

The Square, as we see it today, is the result of an intense building activity protracted along a time span which started in the 13th century by the acquisition of private plots by the Municipality, and continued through a demolition phase, when modest hovels from the High Middle Age were razed and new prestigious buildings were erected as unifying symbols of continuity and greatness of the political, religious and economic powers.

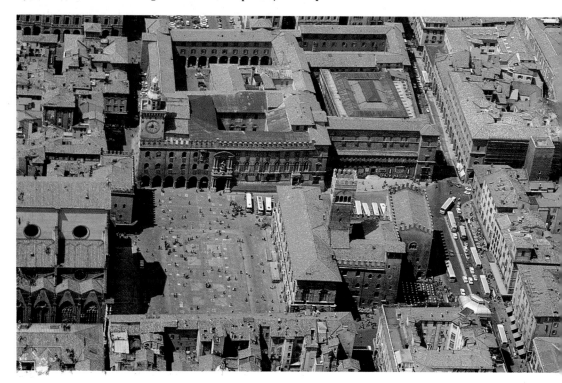

PALAZZO COMUNALE

On the eastern side of the Main Square and of the adjacent Neptune's square stands the imposing structure of the Municipal Palace, commonly known as **Accursius' Palace** because the houses of the Accursi, which were bought by the Municipality in 1287, stood originally on its place. During the Pope's rule the building was also called the *Apostolic Palace* because it was the see of the Cardinal Legates and most of all for having housed the Pisan Antipopes Alexander V Filargo and John XXIII Cossa. The porched part, built along simple, already Gothic, lines over the Accursi's houses, dates back to 1287 while their

---

1. Piazza Maggiore is framed on the east by the Municipal Palace compound. 2. The Municipal Palace: the 12th and 14th century façades linked together by the 16th century portal.

older tower took on its final and still existing shape in 1444. The wing at the right of the big sandstone portal (by Galeazzo Alessi, 1550-1555), to which Fioravante Fioravanti added features typical of the transition period from the Gothic style to the Renaissance, dates back to 1425. The façade looking out on Neptune's square, by Francesco Morandi also called Terribilia dates from 1583. The crenellated cornices and towers, which can still be seen on the southern, western and northern sides, date back to the years 1364-65 and are parts of the fortification works carried out by the Cardinal Legate Androino della Rocca. The clock on the tower was made by Rinaldo Gandolfi in 1773 to replace the one adorned with wooden automata beating the hours made by Giovanni di Evangelista from Piacenza and Bartolomeo di Gnudolo in 1451. Between two windows on the second floor, is placed the extraordinarily plastic *Madonna of the Square*, a large relief terracotta work by Niccolò dell'Arca, dated from 1478 and restored in 1982-83. On the portal by Alessi can be seen the *bronze statue*

1

of Gregory XIII Boncompagni, the Bolognese Pope who reformed the Julian Calendar in 1582. This powerful work by Alessandro Menganti was cast by Anchise Censori in 1576-80. Near the Neptune's statue the *scarp* of the palace keeps still intact slabs of Istrian stone bearing the *old Bolognese measurement gauges*; the monumental sandstone *window*, with tympanum and balcony on half-pilasters, is the work of Alessi (1555) and was restored in 1974; of the two beautiful *eagles* in red marble from Verona, the left one is allegedly attributed to Michaelangel.

On the wall facing Neptune's square under the crenellated passage, monuments commemorating tragic phases of the town's life are to be found: the *Shrine for the dead partisans*, plaques listing the names of people who died in concentration camps, of the victims of terrorism (the bombings on the «Italicus» train in 1974, at the train station on 2 August 1980 and on Christmas time in 1983), and a tablet for Anteo Zamboni who tried to assassinate Mussolini. The southern side of the building is decorated with a beautiful two-mullioned window in the flowery Gothic style of Lombardy.

From the *courtyard of ceremonies* enclosed on three sides by open galleries (dating from 1425-28 and 1508) and a close front built in 1661, let us go to the *Horsemen's Courtyard* at whose centre a modern copy (1934) of the aedicule of the cistern made in 1568 by Francesco Terribilia for the Semplici Garden is placed. The *third courtyard* is what remains of the area of the above-mentioned Garden, on which the Commodity Market stood in 1886. A *stone-ramp* attributed by the tradition to Bramante winds up towards the Hercules' room on the first floor, which is named after the big *statue of Hercules*, a terracotta work made by Alfonso Lombardi in 1518. The famous fresco of the *Madonna of the Earthquake*

painted by Francesco Francia in 1505 hangs on the southern wall of the room. The walled Bologna dotted with towers lying at the feet of the Madonna is the best known representation of the ancient town. From this room we go to the *Hall of the Municipal Council*, whose magnificent vault was frescoed by Colonna and Pizzoli (1674-77), and at whose walls two canvasses by Ubaldo Gandolfi and two marble busts by Giuseppe Mazza (the Hall was restored in 1987-88) are to be found. Another stone-ramp leads to the second floor: a large polychrome terracotta high-relief of the *Madonna with Child and Angels*, once called *Madonna of the Customs House* is to be found on the landing, a work of Camillo Mazza (1667) which comes from the razed Customs house at Porto Naviglio and was brought in the palace in 1937. At one end of the *Farnese Room*, decorated with a cycle of frescoes from the 17th century depicting significant moments in the town's history (Carlo Cignani and Giovanni M. Bibiena are among the authors) is placed a copper *statue of Pope Alexander VII Chigi* by Dorasante d'Osio (1660). A richly-decorated front with sandstone pilaster-strips and half-columns, finished with scagliola during the last century, stands on the southern wall: it is the massive passageway (by Galeazzo Alessi in 1555) opening to the *Farnese or Legate Chapel*. This solemn room roofed by wooden trusses above a grand cornice by Alessi was frescoed around 1562 by Prospero Fontana with *Tales of the Virgin*. Seriously damaged in the early 19th century, when the Chapel was converted into an archive, the magnificent paintings were recently restored to their former glory in the 1980's throung 1992, and today provide a more exact frame of reference for the art of the famous Bolognese painter.

At the end of the Farnese room a marble portal with finely decorated wings leads to the old *Apartment of the Cardinal Legate* which has housed the **Municipal Art Collections** since 1937. It is a very rich collection of works of art established through time thanks to donations and acquisitions.

The most important donations were made by Pelagio Palagi (1860), Cincinnato Baruzzi (1878), Agostino Pepoli (1910), Pietro Giacomo Rusconi and Luisa Verzaglia Rusconi (1919), Carlo Alberto Pizzardi (1922) and Piero Ignazio Rusconi (1930). The Museum was opened in 1937 and its curator Guido Zucchini organized a new layout of the exhibit in 1951. Its rooms, which portray quite aptly the decorative taste of noble families from the 16th to the 18th centuries, are filled with many diverse artworks of great importance. In

---

1. The Clock Tower, renewed in the 15th century. 2. The portal by Galeazzo Alessi (16th century). 3. Gregory XIII, bronze statue by Alessandro Menganti (1580). 4. The Virgin of the Square, a terracotta work by Nicolò dell'Arca (1478).

4

27

this guide we will illustrate only those that seem to us more outstanding.

Room I, called the Swiss room: two 15th-century *Bridal chests* by the workshop of De Marchi family from Crema coming from the Bentivoglio castle; *Portrait of a Lady* by the 17th-century Flemish school; *Portrait of a Commander* by Artemisia Gentileschi, 1622; *Portrait of a Lady* by F. Pourbus. Room II, called the Horsemen room: *Family Scene* by Marcantonio Franceschini; *Perseus and Andromeda* and *Dia-*

4

1. A large window by Alessi (1555). 2. The gorgeous eagles in red marble from Verona on the Alessi window. 3. Monument dedicated to the dead partisans. 4. The Old Fountain by Tommaso Laureti (1565) in via U. Bassi.

29

2

na and Endimione by Ubaldo Gandolfi; *The Holy Family* by Simone Cantarini; *Hercules and the Nemaean Lion*, a terracotta work by Giaco-mo di Maria. Room IV, called Vidonian Gallery, built in 1665 for the Legate Cardinal Pietro Vido-ni: among the beautiful paintings by Donato Cre-ti we would like to name just a few, such as the *Portrait of an Old Man*, *Temperance*, *Resting*

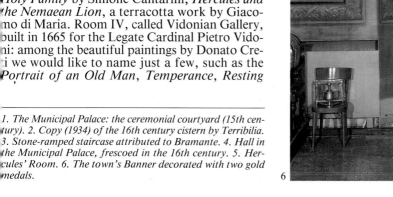

1. The Municipal Palace: the ceremonial courtyard (15th cen-tury). 2. Copy (1934) of the 16th century cistern by Terribilia. 3. Stone-ramped staircase attributed to Bramante. 4. Hall in the Municipal Palace, frescoed in the 16th century. 5. Her-cules' Room. 6. The town's Banner decorated with two gold medals.

6

Woman, Mercury and Paris; the *Capture of King Enzo* by Gaetano Gandolfi; a *Bust of Francesco Pannolini* by Agostino Corsini dating from the 18th century, *Portrait of an Old Man*, the only terracotta work made by Antonio Canova; *Head of an Adolescent*, a marble work by Vincenzo Gemito (1911); *Adonis*, marble work by Cincinnato Baruzzi; *The Damned Man*, bronze by Valentino Brustolon (1894). Room V: *The An-*

nunciation by Jacopo di Paolo; *The Cruficix* by Michele di Matteo; wonderful *Crucifixion* panel by Francesco Francia; *The Saints James and Anthony*, *Saint Paul and a Pilgrim*, panels by Vitale from Bologna (1345); *Saint Woman* by Luca Signorelli. Room VI: *Virgin with Child and Saints* by Innocenzo from Imola; *Portrait of an Old Man* by Jacopo Tintoretto; *Crucifix* by Alessandro Magnasco; *Portrait of a Young Man* by Fra Galgario; *Joseph in Prison* by Guercino; nine frescoes by Bartolomeo Cesi transferred on canvas with *Tales of the Virgin*; the *Annunciation* by Calvaert; *St. Catherine in prison* by Ludovico Carracci. Room VII: *Saints Anthony Abbot and Peter from Alcantara* and a *Portrait of Cardinal Lambertini* by Giuseppe Maria Crespi; *The Death of Cesar* by Vincenzo Camuccini; *The Holy Family* by Gaetano Gandolfi; several paintings of Pelagio Palagi. Room XIII, also called the Sforza Room, with paintings, furniture and ware from the Rusconi collections of which we would like to list the following: *Autumn* and *Winter* by Pier Francesco Cittadini and Jean Boulanger. Room XIV: a collection of 135 Miniatures from different European schools. Room XVII, also called Urbanus's room, built in 1630 for Cardinal Bernardino Spada in honour of Pope Urbanus VIII Barberini, with a splendidly painted ceiling by Agostino Mitelli, Girolamo Curti called Dentone (the extraordinary *trompe-l'oeil* architectural and perspective effects

2

are his) and Angelo Michele Colonna (the three open perspective elements and the *Putti* maybe drawn by Guido Reni); the 188 coats of arms of the Legates who ruled Bologna from 1327 to 1744 are to be found on the walls.

In one of the rooms the painting collection of the John XXIII Institute, a clinic and home for retired people, formed by donations and works previously in the now-suppressed churches of Saints Leonard and Ursula and of St. Gregory of the Beggars, is now permanently exhibited.

1. The Red Room. 2. The Municipal art collections: the Swiss Room. 3. Vitale da Bologna: St. Peter and the pilgrim (14th century). 4. Jacopo di Paolo: Crucifix (14th century). 5. Amico Aspertini: Madonna with child (16th century).

5

1

2

Among the hundred works shown are the following: *Mystical Wedding of St. Catherine* by Bagnacavallo; *Virgin Nursing the Child*, around 1510, and attributed to Amico Aspertini; two *Still Lives* by Pier Francesco Cittadini; *David Anointed King* and *The Death of Saul* by Francesco l'Ange; four canvases with *Saints* by the Gandolfi painters; *St. Anthony Abbot* by Giuseppe Maria Crespi.

The Municipal Art Collections are open to the public from 9 a.m. to 2 p.m. on working days, from 9 to 12,30 on Sundays. On Tuesdays and holidays falling during the week the gallery is closed.

The Farnese Room leads into the rooms which make up the Giorgio Morandi Museum, the largest collection of Morandi's art in the world with 220 works including sixty paintings, eleven watercolours, 56 drawings, 75 etchings, one slab, two terra-cotta statues from the artist's youth, two paintings by Iacopino da Todi and library of art volumes. The celebrated *studio* of the great

Bolognese master (1890-1964) has also been rebuilt, where he worked for decades in his house in via Fondazza 36. This Museum was fundamentally made possible by two donations (in 1991 and 1992) by the artist's sister, Maria Teresa Morandi, to the City of Bologna who thus ensured the city's ownership and enjoyment of the works and memories of her illustrious brother. Other donations and legacies - including other, previous ones by the Morandi family - such as the Cesare Gnudi and Camilla Malvasia legacies, and purchases from the Ingrao and Giuseppe Raimondi collections, had already allowed the formation of a collection in 1987 (in the City Modern Art Gallery), which has now been merged with the collection here.

Luca Signorelli: Head of Saint. 2. Francesco Francia: Crucifixion. 3. Donato Creti: Mercury and Paris. 4. Giuseppe M. Crespi: Cardinal Lambertini (a sketch). 5. Ubaldo Gandolfi: Diana and Endymion.

6

PALAZZO DEL PODESTÀ

At the northern side of Piazza Maggiore and facing St. Petronius Church stands the Palace of the Podestà. The original building, which was listed in old documents under the name of *Palatium Vetus* (old palace), dated back to the 13th century. Since at the end of the 15th century the building was already dilapidated, Giovanni II Bentivoglio, lord of the town, ordered its complete reconstruction based on the project of Aristotele Fioravanti, a Bolognese architect already famous in Eastern Europe for his contribution for the building of the Kremlin Palace in Moscow. In his project Fioravanti had to take into account other important older buildings, that is to say the Arengo tower, the big vault underneath it, a meeting point of four roads, and the adjacent *Palatium Novum* (new palace) called King Enzo's. It was also necessary to include in the new building a hall large enough for the meetings of the Council of the Four Thousand, formed by the thousand representatives of the town's boroughs charged with the attribution of official duties for Bologna and the countryside. Works started in 1485. As we can still see it today, in this building the traditional Medieval architectural criteria are boldly replaced by Renaissance-style solutions: the imposing façade shows a row of ten pilasters rithmically dividing nine large arched windows, all closely topped by corbelling. Nine arches of the arcade held up by a row of Corinthian half columns correspond to the big windows above. In the project by Fioravanti the palace does not seem to block the passage as a heavy barrier but, on the contrary, with the nine arches of its arcade seems to multiply the imaginary lines linking it to the square, a unique interpretation of public open spaces in which buildings do not impinge on the fruition of common property. The decorative elements which cover the palace with vast imaginative solutions are the work of stonecutters from Tuscany. In 1525 the big vault underneath the Arengo tower was embellished by adding terracotta statues modelled by Alfonso Lombardi, dedicated to four patron saints of the town. From 158 to 1767 the Council Hall was used for theatrical representations. In 1604 Pietro Fiorini was commissioned by the Municipality to build a hard stone balustrade along the front: this parapet was built as a protection for people risking to crush down on the square while assisting to quite animated shows such as joustings, ball games or other games.

---

1. The imposing Podestà Palace (15th century). 2. The Arengo Tower (13th century): the Guelph battlements. 3. The Notary Palace, 13th-15th centuries.

In 1639 architect Francesco Rivarola from Ferrara transformed this hall in a real theatre. During the first decades of the 20th century the Council Hall was finally frescoed by Adolfo de Carolis.

PALAZZO DEI NOTAI

The Notary Palace, whose original and oldest nucleous dates back to 1287, stands at the North side of the square. The upgrading works which were carried out in the 14th and 15th centuries bear witness of the great and frenzied building activities which characterized the growth of the Guilds for 27 arts or trades. In particular let us recall that the Notary Guild applied a very rigid admission code for its members who had to have a good starting capital. The palace was at first enlarged on the side looking at St. Petronius's (today's Via Pignattari) by Antonio di Vincenzo. The following enlargement works were allegedly carried out by Bartolomeo Fioravanti in 1422 by keeping to the late-Gothic style and using the Neo-medieval theme of the brickwork decorated two-mullioned windows and the crenellated battlements. Inside the palace remains of the old decorations dating back to the 15th century and some ceilings from the 16th century, painted and coffered, are still visible.

BASILICA DI SAN PETRONIO

St. Petronius was the eighth bishop of the town, he exercised his pastorship from 431 to 450. At his death he was buried in the church of St. Stephen, the same church that he had enriched while alive with a precious reproduction of the Holy Sepulchre in Jerusalem. An apocriphal «biography» of the Saint, written in Latin by a Benedictine monk from St. Stephen in the second half of the 12th century, and a second one in vernacular about a century later attributed to the Saint miraculous merits in the public eyes by portraying him as the founder of the town after an alleged distruction of Bologna ordered by the Emperor Theodosius I and as the founder of the University. It was even easier to make the Saint the symbol of allegiance to the free-town of Bologna, and from 1253, year in which for the first time the representatives of the Municipal Authorities participated in the festivities held in the day dedicated to him (October 4), Saint Petronius has always been looked upon as the chief patron saint of Bologna.

«Wishing to perpetuate, with the help of God, the ancient tradition of liberty and happiness that this august town of Bologna has had for man years, so as to spare us and our children the un bearable yoke of slavery, the heavier and harde after having tested the rich flavour of freedor that God Himself has granted us...so that th guardian and defender of this people and thi town, St. Petronius, be our mediator in th presence of God in the protection, defense, con servation and preservation of our freedom an popular government, ...». Thus with this speacl the General Council of the Six hundreds of th People and free-town of Bologna decreed in 138 the construction of the grand Basilica, the onl place of worship chosen to look on Piazza Mag giore, which was never to become a Cathedra but a religious and civic temple, a real symbc of the Town's most deeply-felt traditions.

On 7th June 1390 the foundation stone wa solemnly laid where the façade now stands. From that date the construction of the church was car ried out under the direction of architect Anto nio di Vincenzo who had drawn the origina project and by 1401, year of his death, two span with four lateral chapels had already beer erected.

Works on the cyclopean site were to last fo

almost another century but the church was never to be completed; another project drawn by architect Arduino Arriguzzi between 1514 and 1516, heavily modifying the original one, was not brought to completion.

Between 1646 and 1658 the vaults on the nave were closed by Francesco Martini following a drawing by Girolamo Rainardi and in 1659, with the completion of the apse, the church took on today's aspect: 132 m. long, 60 m. wide, 44.27 m. high from the keystones of the nave to the floor, and 51 m. high in the façade. Finally on October 3 1954, having dismissed any remaining aspiration to further enlarge it, the Church was consecrated.

The base of the façade was built starting from 1393 and shows in its middle the famous *Porta Magna* (Big Portal) of the Basilica, a real masterpiece of Italian early Renaissance sculpture. In it the Senese sculptor Jacopo della Quercia (1371-1438) carved the tales of man's sins and redemption with his wide-breath and monumental style so much admired even by Michaelangel.

The squared partitions represent: (on the right, in the pilaster-strips) *The Creation of Man*; *The Creation of the Woman*; *The Original Sin*; *The Expulsion from the Garden of Eden*; *The Condemnation to Work*; (on the right) *The Offerings of Cain and Abel to God*; *Cain Slaying Abel*; *Noah, his Family and the Animals Entering into the Ark*; *The Drunken Noah Is Derided by his Sons*; *The Sacrifice of Isaac*; (on the architrave) *The Birth of Jesus*; *The Adoration of the Kings*; *The Presentation of Jesus to the Temple*; *The*

1. The unfinished façade of St. Petronius's marks the southern edge of Piazza Maggiore. 2. St. Petronius's Basilica: the Main Door, a masterpiece by Jacopo della Quercia.

2

2

Slaying of the Innocents; *The Flight to Egypt*.

In the lunette: the highly expressive *Virgin with Child*, one of Jacopo's masterpieces, placed between the Saints *Ambrogio* (later addition by Domenico da Varignana made in 1510) and *Petronius* (by Jacopo).

The smaller door wings were instead made by several sculptors, assembled by the Fabric's Board of the Basilica in order to shorten the time of execution. Amico Aspertini, Nicolò Tribolo, Francesco da Milano, Giacomo Silla, Alfonso Lombardi, Lazzaro Casario, Zaccaria Zacchi, Properzia de Rossi, Ercole Seccadenari, and many others sculpted the tiles, the decoration of

---

1. Main door: Madonna with Child and the Saints Petronius and Ambrose. 2. Left side door (detail), with the Resurrection. 3. Right side door (detail), with the Deposition. 4. Main Door: the Flight into Egypt. 5. Main Door: the Condemnation to work. 6. Main Door: drunken Noah is mocked by Cam.

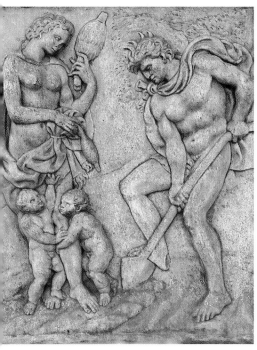

6

pilasters'rows and the well-rounded figures
the lunettes between 1524 and 1530 while the
owning spires were added in 1557 when the
rble coating was still being applied to the fa-
de following the plan by Domenico da Vari-
ana, coating which was never completed.
The themes represented are the following: (on
e pilasters' rows on the left door) *The Tales of
cob, Isaac, Esau, and Lot*; (in the cornice) *The
paritions of Christ after the Resurrection*; (in
e lunette) *The Resurrection of Christ* by Lombardi and his helpers; (on the pilasters' rows on
the right door) *The Tales of Joseph the Hebrew*;
(in the cornice) *The Passion of Christ*; (in the lunette) *Christ Taken down from the Cross* by
Aspertini, between the *Madonna* by Tribolo and
St. John the Evangelist by Seccadenari.

The inside of the church touches and entices
the visitor certainly for its imposing vastness but
even more so for the light which bathes it, for
its special red and white tints, the heraldic colours
of the Bologna City-State, and for the extreme

41

rarefaction of the supporting elements; the space between the columns measures, in fact, fifty Bolognese feet, that is about 19 metres. This feature confers to the structure a uniquely delicate, and at the same time, strong aspect in a show of Gothic forms which, however, have nothing left in them of the Northern verticality.

The lateral chapels which hold rather important artistic documents are an authentic repertory of decorative styles. In the first chapel, dedicated to St. Abbondio (the transenna, altar and glass windows date to 1865-67), two frescoes in which Giovanni da Modena condensed, in 1420, a complete treatise on Medieval theology are to be found on the lateral walls: (on the left) *the effects of Christ's Death on the relations between the Catholic Church and the Jewish Synagogue*; (on the right) *the tree of Good and Evil, instrument of temptation, becomes Christ's cross, instrument of redemption placed across the Old and the New Testament.*

Between this chapel and the next one we find a sandstone cross made by the stonecutters Alberico and his son Pietro and dated 1159. It is one of the four crosses which stood until 1798 on the places where the early-Medieval town's gates once opened.

The second chapel is an example of the richest and most ornate Baroque decoration, erected for Card. Pompeo Aldrovandi who is buried here, by the architect Alfonso Torreggiani between 1720 and 1749. The prone statue of the Cardinal is by Camillo Rusconi from Rome (1727), the other sculptures (Religion and Knowledge) in

wood are works of Ottavio and Nicola Toselli the stucco relief works in the lunettes (*Tables the life of St. Petronius* and *Virtue*); the *Assum tion of the Virgin* on the vault is the work of V torio Bigari and Stefano Orlando.

The niche above the altar contains a preciou *reliquary for the head of St. Petronius* made Rome by Francesco Giardoni and donated to th basilica by Pope Benedict XIV Lambertini.

The third chapel, dedicated to St. Yves, is als in Baroque style but according to the more sobe and shining forms preferred in Bologna. It wa decorated in 1752 on the basis of a design by th arch. Carlo Francesco Dotti, the scultures are b Angelo Gabriello Piò and the altar-piec representing the *Virgin of St. Luke with th Saints Emidio and Yves* is by Gaetano Gandol (1781). A small restoration attempt on the rigl wall has brought to light a portion of the ol decoration (1438-40) made by Giovanni Lianor

The fourth chapel is the only one which ha come to us in its pristine conditions. The decc ration was made between 1400 and 1420 for th wealthy silk merchant Bartolomeo Bolognin Antonio di Vincenzo, the architect of the churcl drew the *transenna* in 1400, while the anonymou sculptor called the «Master of St. Petronius carved the sparkling wood polyptych whose foc part (Tales of the Kings) and the corner colum (*Saints and Prophets*) were painted by Jacopo

1. *Left side of the basilica, looking on to via Archiginnasi* 2. *St. Dominic in the basilica's marble base. 3. The harmoni and luminous inside of St. Petronius's. 4. Giovanni da Mod na: the Crucifix between the Synagogue and the Church. Giovanni da Modena: the Tree of the Cross between the O and New Testament.*

42

5

Paolo from Bologna, who also prepared the cartoons for the stained-glass windows representing: *Christ in His glory, the Annunciation* and *several Saints and the Evangelists*.

Between 1408 and 1420, Giovanni da Modena frescoed the walls, with representations of: on the left, *Heaven and Hell*; on the back, *Tales of St. Petronius' Life*; and on the right, the fantastic *Tales of the Kings*.

The next chapel, dedicated to St. Sebastian, was decorated between 1487 and 1497. The ideals and the stylistic reforms of the Renaissance style are already evident in its forms.

The altar-piece, representing the *Martyrdom of St. Sebastian* with the canon Donato Vaselli who commissioned the decoration works in the chapel, is by an anonymous painter from Northern Italy; the massive *Twelve Apostles* on the side walls are by Lorenzo Costa from Ferrara who painted also the *Annunciated Madonna* at the right-hand side of the altar-piece. The *Annunciating Angel*, instead, is by Francesco Raibolini, also called «Francia».

1. Pietro and Alberico: a stone Cross (1159). 2. The Baroque St. Petronius's Chapel. 3. Bolognini Chapel, decorated in the years 1400-1420. 4. Wood polyptych painted by Jacopo di Paolo.

45

2

1. Giovanni da Modena:
detail of the painted cycle
of the Kings 2 detail of the
ceramic floor (1487). 3. St.
Sebastian Chapel: the
stained-glass windows
designed by Costa (15th
century). 4. St. James
Chapel, with its magnifi-
cent altar-piece by Costa.
5. St. James Chapel: tomb
of the Baciocchi princes
(19th   century).

4

The refined intarsia which decorate the *kneeling stools and the benches* with intricatedly
woven designs are by Giacomo di Agostino 'de'
Marchi (1495) and the ceramic *floor* is a real
masterpiece made by Pietro di Andrea from
Faenza in 1487.

The stained-glass windows representing *St. Sebastian*, the *Annunciation* and the *Patron Saints
of Bologna* are maybe the works of the master
glass-makers Cabrini following a drawing by
Costa.

The next chapel, the sixth one, is characterized
by a modern art work, the bronze statue of
Cardinal Giacomo Lercaro, by Giacomo Manzù, placed there to celebrate the solemn consecration of the Basilica (1954).

In the seventh chapel, dedicated to St. James,
there is a very ornate transenna attributable to
the school of Francesco di Simone from Fiesole
(end of 15th century) and contemporary to the
magnificent altar-piece (*The Enthroned Virgin
with Child between the Saints Sebastian, James,
Jerome and George*), the masterpiece of Lorenzo Costa (1492).

We should also mention the *sepulchral monument* on the right-hand side of the chapel. It contains the mortal remains of Prince Felice Baccioc-
chi and his wife Elisa Bonaparte, Grand-Duchess
of Tuscany and sister of Napoleon I, and is the
refined work by Cincinnato Baruzzi (the three big
statues) and by Lorenzo Bartolini (the base, the

5

moulding and the exquisite Elisa's portrait on the side).

The line of St. Petronius's famous sun-dial, traced by Domenico Cassini in 1655 and restored by Eustachio Zanotti in 1765, starts here. It is the biggest sun-dial ever built in a closed area and its length is exactly a six-hundred-thousandth of one of the Earth's meridians.

In the following chapels the following works stand out for their historical and artistic importance: *St. Rocco's Ecstasy* a touching and intense work by Francesco Mazzola also called «Parmigianino» (1527) is in the eighth one; *The Archangel Michael* noble and impetuous in this representation by Denjs Calvaert (1582) is in the ninth, while in the eleventh you can see the two large flanks of the 14th-century organ, decorated with *scenes from the life of St. Petronius* by Amico Aspertini (1531) who applied to it his usual daring and non-conformist style. They were covered by Baroque decorations in the 17th century and only after recent restoration works were they brought to light.

The museum of the Basilica is to be found at the end of the nave. It is rather small but none the less very interesting, not only for its sacred apparel, the miniated manuscripts, and the sculptures but also for its rich collection of drawings made for the façade of the church by many great architects such as Baldassarre Peruzzi, Vignola, Palladio and others.

The main chapel and the apse of the churc were completely restructured between 1653 an 1663.

The great *tribune* over the altar was enlarge in 1673 according to a drawing by the Archite Gian Giacomo Monti. It is decorated with exqu site stucco works by Giovanni Battista Barbe ni for the figures and by Paolo Griffoni for t ornamentations. Later on these artists ma (1674-75) the massive Baroque cover for the o gans, that is the instruments which are some the most outstanding masterpieces of t Basilica.

The *organ at the right*, built by Lorenzo di Gi como from Prato between 1471 and 1475, is t oldest big organ which has kept its original sta and the first to have independent stops. The o gan at the left was added by Baldassarre Malan ni in 1596 and from then on the music for S Petronius's was composed to be played on tw opposite organs. Therefore, the musical chap of the church came to be known as one of t best in Italy for over two centuries.

1. The famous line meridian by Cassini. 2. St. Roch, by P migianino. 3. The imposing pulpit and the 15th and 16 century organs.

48

2

The large wooden Crucifix from the 15th century hanging over the altar is very imposing as the choir carved by Agostino de' Marchi between 1467 and 1479. For the two central stalls he used the drawings of the famous painter Francesco del Cossa from Ferrara.

Museum of St. Petronius: wood model of the Basilica (16th century). 2. An ivory reliquary. 3. Astylar Cross. 4. 15th-century Miniature. 5. 15th-century Miniature. 6. Large reliquary in precious metals and semiprecious stones.

6

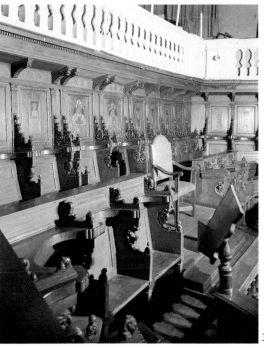

A false grotto opens up on the outer side un
der the right organ. In it you can find the large
Pietà a polychrome terracotta work made by Vin
cenzo Onofri at the beginning of the 16th cen
tury.

The second side chapel when walking down the
right aisle is the one which belonged to the old
Guild of the Beccai (Butchers) and contains the
scintillating altar-piece with the *Virgin in Glory
between the Saints Petronius and Dominic*, a
peculiar work by Bartolomeo Passarotti who
painted it around 1580.

The third chapel is a good example of full
Renaissance decorations. It was made between
1524 and 1526 by Girolamo da Treviso, who is
also the author of the statue representing *St. An
thony* and the monochrome paintings on the
walls depicting the *Miracles of the Saint*, for the
wealthy Bolognese merchant Giovanni Antonio
Saraceni.

The stained-glass windows are quite interest
ing: in the big rose-window (*St. Anthony*) as well
as in the small ones (*The Annunciation*), based
on the cartoons made by Perugino around 1518,
the serene linearity so typical of the 15th centu
ry is markedly evident while in the eight large

*1. The tribune of the High-Altar: 17th-century decoration.
2. Wood Crucifix from the 15th century. 3. Wood inlay choir
by Agostino de' Marchi, 1469-79. 4. The precious organ by
Lorenzo da Prato, 1471-75.*

MUNICIPALITY OF BOLOGNA

Sala del Consiglio Comunale (già Galleria del Senato)
Municipal Council Hall (formerly Senate Gallery)

The Senators' Gallery in Bologna was frescoed in 1676 by Angelo Michele Colonna (1604-1687) with the help of Gioacchino Pizzoli (1651-1731). This is a splendid example of Baroque art and the typical inside decoration which made Bologna school famous throughout the world: the quadratura, where the skilled use of perspective opens up to illusory views and landscapes. The architectural quadratura covera a 34 m-long and 8.5 m-wide area.

Four painted columns support the mock moulding, thus creating the illusion of supporting another vaulted ceiling composed of five allegorical scenes, making reference to Bologna's virtues.

The first shorter wall of the hall depicts the town Coat of arms supported by two Virtues (Concord and Loyalty) together with the symbols of local and papal powers.

The central vault depicts: 1) Minerva (goddess of knowledge) and Mars (god of warfare) convince Fame to announce the town's virtues to the world. 2) Cybele points out to Bologna (depicted as a woman on a lion-driven cart, symbolising strength and power) the glory of Olympus where Jupiter is waiting for her. 3) Bacchus, Pomona and Caeres (referring to wine, fruit and harvest) are the symbols of the fertile soil of Bologna.

In the second shorter wall: Vigilance and Prudence and the symbols of the arts.

COMUNE DI BOLOGNA

Sala del Consiglio Comunale
(già Galleria del Senato)

La Galleria dei Senatori di Bologna fu affrescata nel 1676 da Angelo Michele Colonna (1604-1687), con l'aiuto del giovane Gioacchino Pizzoli (1651-1731). E' uno splendido testo d'arte barocca e tipico esempio di una tipologia di decorazione di interni che rese famosa la scuola bolognese nel mondo: la quadratura, dove l'uso sapiente della prospettiva apre le superfici su illusori spazi aperti. La quadratura architettonica occupa la volta per 34 metri di lunghezza e 8,50 di larghezza.

Quattro colonne dipinte sostengono il finto cornicione e creano l'illusione di sostenere una nuova volta; in cui si aprono cinque scene figurate di soggetto allegorico, con riferimento alle virtù di Bologna.

Nel primo lato breve è raffigurato lo *Stemma* della città sorretto da due *Virtù* (*Concordia* e *Fedeltà*) insieme ai simboli del potere locale e di quello pontificio.

Nella volta centrale: 1) *Minerva* (dea della Sapienza) *e Marte* (dio della guerra) inducono la fama ad annunciare al mondo le virtù e le glorie della città. 2) *Cibele* indica a *Bologna* (con sembianze femminili, sul carro trainato da due leoni a simboleggiare la potenza) la gloria dell'Olimpo dove Giove l'attende. 3) *Bacco, Pomona e Cerere* (alludenti al vino, ai frutti e alle messi) simboleggiano la fertilità della terra bolognese.

Nel secondo lato breve: *Vigilanza e Prudenza* e i simboli delle arti.

1

figures of Saints made in the second half of the same century from a drawing by Pellegrino Tibaldi an exuberant plasticism, forerunner of the Baroque style, leaves its mark.

In the next chapel, dedicated to the *Holy Sacrament*, the following works should be mentioned: the gorgeous intarsia on the side stools made by the Olivetan fra Raffaele da Brescia between 1513 and 1521 for the church of St. Michael in the Woods, from which they were taken, and the canopy for the display of the Holy Sacrament in precious marbles made in Rome after the design of Alessandro Algardi in 1633.

The fifth chapel, dedicated to *Immaculate*, represents the last large decorative work carried out in the Basilica. It was built in Art Nouveau style between 1908 and 1929 (the last additions and touches date back to 1951) from a drawing by Achille Casanova. The paintings are by Casanova and Renato Pasqui, the floor by the Chini House from Tuscany (1918) and the screen by Armando Casadio (1929).

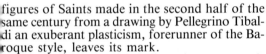

1. Bartolomeo Passarotti: Virgin with the Saints Petronius and Dominic. 2. Girolamo da Treviso: St. Anthony of Padua, in marble. 3. Holy Sacrament Chapel: the Temple, an intarsia work by Raffaele da Brescia. 4. Holy Sacrament Chapel: St. Petronius, an intarsia work by Raffaele da Brescia.

2

In the remaining chapels we should at least recall: the altar-piece of the seventh chapel, a «scary» *Pietà* painted by Amico Aspertini in 1519 with an incredibly dramatic expressiveness; in the next one, dedicated to the *Holy Cross*, which belonged to the Notary Guild, the refined transenna made between 1481 and 1483 in the workshop of Albertino Rusconi from Ferrara, and the famous window made by the Blessed Dominican James from Ulm (Jacob Griesinger) from a drawing by Michele di Matteo in 1464-66, which astounds us for its bright polychromy and its pellucid colours.

Amico Aspertini: a dramatic Pietà. 2. Lorenzo Costa: St. Jerome. 3. Holy Cross Chapel: stained-glass windows by James from Ulm (15th century). 4. Piazza Maggiore: the Banchi Palace by Vignola.

PALAZZO DEI BANCHI

As regards the eastern side of the square, we can see another architectural intervention over previously existing buildings: the Palace of Banchi. In 1565 Jacopo Baruzzi called Vignola was called upon to solve a difficult problem in the square's layout. He was to «hide» the picturesque array of Medieval shops and hovels all huddled up together, thus conferring upon the square a new dignity while keeping the link with the noisy Pescherie and Clavature alleyways untouched. Barozzi adopted a sort of theatrical artifice by creating a prestigious backdrop, that is the front of the building is made of a continuous row of fifteen spans on two tiers. The lower tier is an arcade spatiated by Corinthian pilaster strips, and through its two big archways the access to the market is left intact. The upper tier had to be adapted according to the style of the surrounding buildings, all with windows at different levels. Therefore the Palace of Banchi is considered a magnificent feat considering its perfectly harmonius structure.

Piazza del Nettuno

The name of Neptune's Square, found in documents from the 18th century onward, comes from the monumental fountain, completed in 1566, which stands right where there once was a cluster of houses and shops.

The **Fountain of Neptune** was planned by Tommaso Laureti in 1563, who asked the Flamish sculptor Jean Boulogne from Douai, also called Giambologna, to cast the statue of the sea god in bronze. The representation of the god Neptune follows at once several viewpoints: the model was inspired by the human body in movement and the statue is permeated by a spiral-like motion, which seems to invite the viewer to look around it in order to see it in its full complexity. Most of the weight of the god who is holding a trident rests on its left foot while the right one is on the back of a dolphin. The square base stands out for its red Verona marble against the whiteness of the marble basin. A complex allegory of the world's four main rivers flowing down at sea is represented by introducing mythological symbols and devices: putti playing with

1

58

dolphins, small shell-shaped basins, mermaids, mascarons, and lion-headed protomes. In the pedestal we can see the coats of arms of the Pope and of the papal deputy legate but the main justification for this work is the celebration of Pius IV and his enlightened rule.

halls of the mezzanine and of the first floor were used for great popular gatherings. If we turn right from Neptune's square we come to the street once known as Middle Market which, after having gone through a complete uplifting in 1889, is now called via Rizzoli.

PALAZZO DI RE ENZO

On Neptune's square at the right-hand of the fountain, we come to King Enzo's Palace, which dates from 1244. In this building, destined in the beginning to house the Town's Council, King Enzo, son of Frederick II, was kept until his death (1272) after having been defeated and taken prisoner by the Bolognese at the battle of Fossalta (1249). The restoration works carried out by Alfonso Rubbiani (1905-1913) have made it possible for us to have an idea of its medieval aspect: he added a row of battlements and two three-light windows but most of all he razed buildings dating back to the 16th century in order to open up again the palace old·courtyard. In the ground floor of the palace, once covered by cross-vaults, war engines were kept while the big

1. A romantic view of the Neptune fountain. 2. Night scene: the Neptune fountain and the «curia protestatis». 3. Neptune square with the King Enzo and Podestà Palaces. 4. The imposing and renowned Fountain by Jean de Boulogne.

2

1. The Podestà and King Enz
Palaces: their animated ou[t]
lines. 2. The Podestà's cour[t]
yard or «curia potestatis».

Via Rizzoli

In its picturesque side streets it is still possible to find remains of the oldest Bologna: in via Caduti di Cefalonia (2nd side-street to the left) the 14th-century **Casa Castellani** (ns. 3-5) with its jutting first floor supported by wooden beams and in via Oberdan (3d side-street to the left) **Casa Felicini** (n. 16), **Casa Dalle Corregge** (n. 18), **Casa Beroaldi** (n. 22), and **Casa Buoi** (n. 24) all dating back to the 15th century. At the end of Via Rizzoli we come to piazza di Porta Ravegnana where the **Palazzo dei Drappieri (n. 1)** stands. In 1486 the Cloth-merchants' Guild (Drappieri) commissioned to Giovanni Piccinini from Como the building of their seat, which came to be called, rather vulgarly, «the Rag Palace» by the Bolognese populace. The Guild had demanded that the windows be like the ones from the palace of Giovanni II Bentivoglio, which had been destroyed in 1507: therefore, this building is for us a precious evidence of the architectural ideas prevailing during the Seigneury in the Renaissance period. The façade seems partly shaded by the pilaster-strips which divide the front in even and vertical rows; the balcony is a later addition from the 17th century.

IN THE ANCIENT GHETTO

The mesh of narrow streets, only partially covered by porticos, with its three main axes in the parallel streets via dei Giudei, via dell'Inferno and via Mandria, was the *Ghetto* of the Jews in Bologna («ghetto» derives from the Venetian «ghetto» or «jet», which was the name of a neighborhood of metal foundries inhabited by Jews). Here they were concentrated for the first time in 1366 from the other neighborhoods, located near S. Stefano and in the area S. Vitale - Caldarese - Casteltialto. Their rich history is documented in Bologna beginning in the 12th century. This ghetto, which extended along the two banks of the Aposa (the stream was covered here only in 1462) was practically imprisoned among six churches (S. Giobbe, S. Nicolò degli Albari, Ss. Simone e Giuda, S. Maria dell'Aposa, S. Donato, S. Marco) and one entered through two *vaults*, the Malvasia vault in via Zamboni and the Tubertini vault in via Oberdan, whose wooden doors were bolted at dusk; later two more entrances were added, one in via Giudei near the Two Towers, the other at the Spada Vault in Piazza S. Martino. In 1556 the prolegate Lenzi, executing an order by Paul IV, forced the Jews into the Ghetto once again; they remained there until 1569, and then again from 1586 to

---

1. via Rizzoli, from the east. 2. Ravegnana Square: the Drapers' Palace (15th century).

1

The ancient Ghetto today is part of a cultural project to restore and revitalize the city by inserting shops and craft workshops. The Medieval environment is quiete picturesque, with the fourteenth-century Ugozzoni Tower flanked by an overpass.

1593. In the latter year an edict by Clement VIII drove them definitively out of Bologna (other expulsions had taken place in the past) with the order to concentrate in the ghettos of Ferrara, Cento and Lugo, or to leave the Church State forever. Some of the suggestive street names in the area (via dei Giudei, called *Giudea* since 1556, and vicolo Mandria, which in the 17th century was still called *via del Ghetto*) recall their presence; others, such as *via dell'Inferno*, where they had tripe factories, the alleys *Purgatorio* and *Limbo* which retain their names today, and the streets *via del Carro* and *via Valdonica* have origins which are still the subject of controversy. At number 16 of via dell'inferno, standing tall above heavy corbels, is the *Synagogue House*. In the part of the apse (called aron, custody of the law tables) you can recognize the ancient construction of the 17th century. The entrance was in the parallel alley-lane Mandria. Once left the Jews, the rich family Buratti took possession of the building and was used as habitation.

At number 20/2, a commemorative stone laid on the fiftieth anniversary of the famous «racial laws» of 1938 recalls the Jews of the past (the famous Talmud scholar Obadià Sforno, who founded a Rabbinic school in Bologna in the 15th century, and the no less famous Bolognese scholars Azaria de' Rossi, Yaakov Mantino and Samuel Archivolti who taught there; as well as the Rabbi Alberto Avraham Orvieto and all the other Jews who, along with him, were victims of the 1943 deportations).

LE DUE TORRI

Right from the square of Ravegnana gate we can admire the very symbols of Bologna: the Two Towers. The town's Medieval representational plan is to be perceived in a three-dimensional way, in which verticality has a fundamental role. The towers played mostly a military role not only in the town itself but also in the surrounding countryside, by sending and receiving light messages in case of danger. They were connected to the houses or also to each others through suspended scaffolding. The **Asinelli Tower** was allegedly built between 1109 and 1119 for the Asinelli family. From its slanted base, covered by rusticated gypsum ashlars, the tower rises for 97.20 m. terminating in a small turret with Guelph battlements while its walls are made of two layers of bricks pasted with mortar and pebbles, according to the «dry masonry» technique which was used in Bologna up to the 16th century. In 1488 a sort of bartizan, a square-shaped fortified structure to house the soldiers' watch, was added to the base: it was also used as a temporary prison for noisy night revellers. The inside staircase was built in 1684. In the course of time the Asinelli tower has withstood earthquakes and fire: it has undergone many restoration works and it is now checked one a year. The **Garisenda** tower, which is 47 m. high, dates also back to the 12th century. It is heavily leaning due to a sagging of the ground; even Dante Alighieri recalled it in the canto XXXI of his famous Inferno (verses 136-138) in which he made the well-known similitude regarding the tower. You could try to repeat the experience mentioned by the poet: when a cloud goes by the tower and you follow it from below, it seems that it is the tower which is moving. Stendhal was also right when he said that a Bolognese far away from his town could burst into tears just by thinking of his beloved towers: today also the «heart» of the Petronians, thus the Bolognese are called after their Patron Saint, beats around the Two Towers, which are the poles of radiating streets almost converging at the foot of the Garisenda and Asinelli.

Via dell'Inferno, «axis» of the Ghetto. 2. Memory of the cases and deportations of Jewishes. 3. The risky steepness of the Two Towers. 4. The Garisenda with the «radials» Giudei, Zamboni, S. Vitale.

Piazza della Mercanzia

Once the Mercanzia (Trade)'s square was called the *Carrobbio* (crossroads) to designate the point in which many town's streets came to merge. In this important area of the town centre the **Palazzo della Mercanzia** was built according to a design by Antonio di Vincenzo and Lorenzo from Bagnomarino between 1384 and 1391. The red-brick masonry face enhances with its deep colour the white-stone decorative elements: the balcony surmounted by a spiry canopy and the Istrian stone moulding of the two-light windows are knowingly matched to the terracotta decorations. The frieze below the battlement shows the symbol of the Guilds. The niches held the precious statues of *Justice* and the *Patron Saints of the city*, now in the Civic Medieval Museum. The palace was heavily damaged during and air raid (1943). During the restoration work painstakingly carried out by the Architect Alfredo Barbacci, the replacing parts were marked by a sign so as to allow the identification of the type of intervention and its date even after a long time. On the walls along the inside staircase the coats of arms of the families whose members became Judges in the Merchants' Court can be seen. In this Court, hearings were held on lawsuits and

disputes among buyers and sellers. In the Mercanzia's square we can also see several examples of Medieval houses: the **Case Seracchioli** (Mercanzia's Square n. 3 and via Santo Stefano n. 2) from the 13th century and partly rebuilt in the first decades of the 20th century, **Casa Reggiani** (n. 2) whose brick front has small ogee windows and **Casa Volta** (n. 1) from the 16th century with projection and a roof-terrace.

4

---

1. The clock of Mercanzia (19th century). 2. The refined Mercanzia Palace dates back to the 14th century. 3. The old Carobbio seen from the south. 4. Romanesque abodes, beyond the Merchants' Loggia.

Via Castiglione

Some old chroniclers explained the origin of this street's name from *castilio* or «castel leone», thus relating it to the mountain keep of Castiglione ruled by the Pepoli family from 1340 to the Napoleonic era (1796) and in fact the Pepoli family had owned houses in this street starting from the 13th century. The oldest **Palazzo Pepoli** (ns. 6-8-10) seems almost a castle because of its strong scarp base and the battlements' crowning. The decorative elements are mostly geometrically patterned; note the lancet arch of the portal (n. 6), surmounted by a chess-board, the armourial bearing of the family. The colour of the bricks, now darkly hued, enhance the Medieval atmosphere of the inner courtyard over which massive merlons stand tower-like. The palace, built in 1344 for Taddeo Pepoli, had 200 bedrooms: in fact, more than 180 servants of the Pepoli lived in it. It seems that the lands and estates of this noble family were so vast that 3,800 farmers were not enough to cultivate them all. In via Castiglione n. 7 we find **Palazzo Pepoli Campogrande** which is a brick and sandstone Baroque building, once called «New Pepoli Palace» or «Pepoli of Chains» for the outside fencing with chains and wooden poles. It was erected for Odoardo Pepoli in front of the old 14th century abodes between 1660 and 1709. The Architect Giovanni Battista Albertoni (front looking ont via Castiglione), Giovanni Giacomo Monti (ha and stair-case), Giuseppe Antonio Torri (fron on via Clavature), Francesco Angelini (gallery i the «piano nobile») worked on it. The gran stair-case, whose vault was frescoed by Domenic Maria Canuti, leads to the first floor (piano no bile), now owned by the State: we find here ric rooms often covered with marvelous frescoe from the 17th and 18th centuries (*Medieva Pomps of the Pepoli*, and *Hercules in the Olym pus* by Canuti, *Allegory of the Seasons*, *Triump of Hercules*, *The Assembly of the Gods* b Giuseppe M. Crespi, 1691, *Alexander and th Gordian Knot* by Donato Creti, 1708). Th **Didactic Section of the National Picture Galler** is housed (see pag. 152) there and many impor tant art shows are held there together with th permanent exhibition of paintings from its valu able *Zambeccari collection*, a private collection from the 18th century which was donated to th State in 1884.

If we go through via Farini, we come acros some interesting buildings: **Palazzo Guastavilla ni** (ns. 20-22) from the 16th century, which show the successful device of two Renaissance porche

3

...ourtyards; **Palazzo Cospi** (n. 21) decorated by ... perspective scene in the 16th century courtyard ...nade by Angelo Michele Colonna, who decorat-...d also the stair-case and the halls with paintings ...epresenting *Allegories of the Cospi family* and ...ne *Sun brought in triumph by the first six hours ...f the day*; **Palazzo Ratta** (n. 24) with the fres-...oes dedicated to Felsina by Burrini; the 15th-...entury **Casa Poeti** (n. 25) whose plan is by tra-...ition attributed to the famous Aristotele Fiora-...anti; **Palazzo Spada** (ns. 25-27) originally from ...ne 16th century, as it is clearly visible in the log-...ia surmounted by architraves in one of the ...ourtyards following the style of Formigine. It ...as then rebuilt in 1764 by Francesco Tadolini ...nd the rooms of the «piano nobile», which are ...ow part of the Hunting Club, were elegantly ...ecorated by artists from the 19th century.

Former Church of Saint Lucia. In here once ...ood the house in which the famous jurist An-...onio da Budrio (1338-1408) had lived and the ...ld parish church of St. Lucia in which St. Fran-...s Xavier stayed as a guest for a few months in ...537.

Via Castiglione: old Pepoli Palace (14th century). 2. Pepoli ...mpogrande Palace (17th century). 3. Cospi Palace (14th ...ntury). 4. Church of St. Lucia (17th century), now the ...niversity's ceremonial assembly hall.

4

1

2

In 1562 the church was bought by the Jesuits who had it completely rebuilt between 1622 and 1659, according to the grand design of Architect Girolamo Rainaldi.

A century after the building, the church's length was to be further touched up according to the design of Architect Francesco Maria Angelini (1686-1731), but the works were never carried beyond the base of the new apse.

The church passed to the Barnabites in 1773 and was later suppressed in the 19th century when it came to be mostly used as a gymnasium and a laboratory. Today, finally free of scaffolding and perfectly restored in 1986-88, S. Lucia has become the Aula Magna of the University. In-

augurated by Pope John Paul II on 7 June 1988 in was the site of the most solemn celebration for the 900th anniversary of the University. I often hosts high-level artistic and cultural events

The adjacent suppressed convent of the Bar nabites still shows its magnificent porch erecte according to the design of Architect Agostin Barelli in 1676, and the very elegant library erec ed in 1742 by Architect Giovan Antonio Am brosi.

Next to the **Torresotto** (12th-13th centuries which was one of the ancient gates opening o to the Medieval walls encircling the town an known as the Walls of the year «one-thousand» stands **Casa Dalla Lana** (n. 47) which in the 15t century belonged to the Wool Trade and wa used as dye-workshop. The wool-making trad had been present in the town of Bologna sinc around 1230 and in its more flourishing perio employed up to 15,000 people in Bologna and th outskirts. The wool workers lived right in this sec tion of town, in Borgo Orfeo, in via degli Ange li and Fiaccalcollo, now via Rialto. The clot which had been made and dyed was dried in th sun by placing it in special open rooms calle «chiodare».

At the end of the street we reach **Port Castiglione**, whose primitive construction datin back to the 13th century was heavily modifie between the end of the 14th century and the be ginning of the 15th century. The gate stands alon because the razing of the walls at the sides of th gateway was decided and carried out in 1902

After the gate and across the tree-lined avenue we come to the **Giardini Margherita** which ca also be reached through Santo Stefano's Gate The *Passeggio Queen Margherita* (Promenade

1. *Torresotto of Castiglione (12th-13th centuries). Castiglione Gate (14th century). 3. Margherita Gardens: t pond. 4. Margherita Gardens: the pond. 5. Church of S. M ria della Misericordia (15th-16th centuries).*

day's Margherita's Gardens, was inaugurated
1879. The project for the landscaping and the
yout of the grounds, with pathways for walk-
g, panoramic views on large sloping meadows,
rub bushes and the pond was made by the
ount of Sambuy who had just terminated the
orks for the Valentino's Gardens in Turin. Dur-
g the landscaping works on the 55 hectares of
nd, tombs of an Etruscan necropolis located in
e Eastern reaches of the Felsina settlement were
ought to light (1876). For educational purposes
e first tomb was disassembled and remounted
1 the field of the old riding-track, where it is
ill possible to see it. The wrought-iron entrance
te, designed by Filippo Antolini (1845), was
iginally part of the Gregorian screen in the
hurch of Saint Stephen. *The equestrian monu-*
ent dedicated to Victor Emmanuel II (by Giu-
) Monteverde, 1888) was once in Piazza Mag-
ore.

Chiesa di S. Maria della Misericordia (Porta
astiglione, 4). In 1431, the Cistercian Sisters
ho had ruled over the church since the 13th cen-
iry left it and the church was taken by the Olive-
n Benedictine Brothers who commissioned the
largement of the choir before abandoning it in
eir turn in 1454.

In 1473 the church who had then a single nave
as acquired by the Augustinian Brothers who
arted a great reconstruction work by raising the
sles and the chapels on the left before 1511, year

5

in which the mercenary troops of the Bentivoglio
family in their attack to the town chased the
Brothers from the church and heavily damaged it.

When peace returned, the façade was rebuilt
and enlarged and the work for the raising of the
vaults was started from the right aisle and
chapels. However, the project stopped there, as
we can still see and therefore the church is a kind
of compromise between the late-Gothic and
Renaissance styles.

Many of the notable paintings in the church
were taken away during the Napoleonic period

69

and are now found in museums in Bologna, Milan and Paris.

Two small stained-glass windows by Francesco Raibolini called «Francia» are, however, still there. They represent the *Virgin with Child* in the second chapel on the right and *St. John the Baptist* in the next sixth chapel, in which a canvas by Gaetano Gandolfi (1734-1802), the *Annunciation*, is also to be found.

The works made by Matteo Cossich, also called the «German» but of Istrian origins, for this church around 1625 are very impressive: th big *tabernacle held up by four Doctors of th Church* now placed over the baptistery; the *choi* and the elaborate *organ's sound box* over th main door.

The *St. Rocco* and a *St. John the Nepomucen* by Giuseppe Maria Crespi (1664-1747) and a *Vir gin with Child between the Saints Sebastian an Orsola* by Vincenzo Spisanelli (1595-1662) ar also quite notable art works.

Piazza dei Tribunali - Via Garibaldi

If we turn right from the square of Castiglione Gate, we come to VIALE XII GIUGNO, planned by Alfonso Rubbiani in 1904 and if we continue along we reach PIAZZA DEI TRIBUNALI where a masterpiece of the 16th-century architecture stands: **Palazzo Ruini** later on Ranuzzi palace (n. 4), today's **Palazzo di Giustizia** (Court's Hall). The project for the massive façade goes back to Andrea Palladio but in the construction, which ended in 1584, the original de-

sign was probably distorted, at least in part. Th central section, evenly spaced by eight Corinthia pilaster strips, is crowned by a tympanum, wit double pyramids at each side, at whose centre th coat of arms is placed, supported by two winge figures. In the last decades of the 17th centur the palace was repeatedly enlarged and the buil ing of the two-flight stair-case, later on decora ed by Filippo Balugani (1770), was initiated. I side the palace we can admire two cycles of pain

igs of relevant iconographic importance: the *Allegory of Fortune* and the *Four Seasons*, frescoed by Marcantonio Franceschini in 1680 in collaboration with the quadraturista painter Enrico Haffner; the *Tales of the Bagni della Porretta* painted by Vittorio M. Bigari in the Gallery (1724-25); the *Tales of Theseus*, *Psyche* and *Fame* signed and dated Felice Giani, 1822.

BASILICA SANTUARIO DI S. DOMENICO

In 1219 a group of Preaching Brothers led by the Blessed Reginald of Orléans moved from the Mascarella church, where they had been temporarily housed, to the small church of St. Nicolò of the Vineyards located among the vineyards and gardens in the outskirts of Bologna.

During that same year, St. Dominic Guzman, the founder of the order, settled in the church where he held the first two General Chapters of the order and, after his death in August 6th 1221, was buried.

At once, the Preaching (or Dominican) Brothers started the complete renewal of the building which was enlarged. It was then consecrated by Pope Innocent IV in 1251 and dedicated to St. Dominic (canonized in 1234 by Pope Gregory IX).

The big basilica was rigidly divided into two parts by a tall wall, one reserved for the brothers (the one towards the altar, where the choir was located), the other for the faithful. Pretty soon the classes for Law students were moved there from the nearby Benedictine church of St. Proculus which had alredy become insufficient.

In the following centuries the two sections of the church were heavily modified by the opening up of side chapels and various restructuration works. These changes became even more evident when the dividing wall (iconostasis) was pulled down in the beginning of the 17th century and the choir was moved behind the altar.

For this purpose the Brothers commissioned the complete renewal of the church's inside to Architect Carlo Francesco Dotti. He terminated the work aimed at masking the eccessive length of the church be devising interrupted and transversal lines between 1727 and 1732.

In the square, still paved with river pebbles according to the Medieval usage common in Bolo-

---

Ranuzzi-Ruini Palace, today's Court Hall, by Palladio (16th century). 2. The evocative cobblestone Square of S. Domenico with St. Dominic's Basilica.

gna, we can admire: the brickwork column raised in 1627 and surmounted by a *copper statue of St. Dominic*, which was made in Milan; the tombs of Rolandino de' Passeggeri, the famous master at Law and Corrector of the Notary Company, terminated by Giovanni, the marble carver, in 1305, and of Egidio Foscherari, built in 1289 by using a Greek marble arch with relief works dating back to the 9th century; the other column in marble, bricks and copper, raised in 1632 after a design by Guido Reni for celebrating the end of the terrible plague which had decimated the population of the town reducing it by a quarter.

The 13th-century façade (restored in 1909 by the architect Raffaele Faccioli) is joined to the large Ghisilardi chapel, built along serene Renaissance lines by Architect Baldassarre Peruzzi from Siena in the beginning of the 16th century.

The church has a collection of historical documents and sacred art objects, which is exceptional in number and quality.

Along the left aisle we can admire: at the third altar, *St. Raimond from Pennafort Plowing the Waves on his Mantle* painted by Ludovico Carracci (1555-1619); in the lateral vestibule, the *tomb of the jurist Alessandro Tartagni* by Francesco di Simone from Fiesole (1477); in the large chapel of the Virgin, the famous *Mysteries of the Rosary* around the niche were painted in 1599-1600 by the best painters of that time working in town such as Ludovico Carracci, Ba tolomeo Cesi, Denjs Calvaert, Lavinia Fontan Guido Reni, Francesco Albani and Domenic Zampieri (called Domenichino), while the bree frescoes on the vault are by Angelo Miche Colonna and Agostino Mitelli (1657); in hei Guido Reni and Elisabetta Sirani are buried; tl tenth chapel (in the transept), the only one have kept intact the original Gothic lines, holc the imposing *Crucifix*, signed by Giunta Pisar (1250), which represents one of the highest e ample of Italy's 13th-century painting, befoi Cimabue.

Moving to the right aisle we can admire: in tl first small chapel besides the Main one, the *My tical Wedding of St. Catherine*, an importai panel by Filippino Lippi (1501) and, at the er of the transept, *St. Thomas Aquinas* by Guerc no (1591-1660).

From the nearby sacristy (on the altar, a *N tivity* by Luca Cambiaso from Genoa, 1527-158 we can reach the small museum (where we ca

3

find: a terracotta *Bust of St. Dominic* by Nicolò dell'Arca, 1474; fragments of a terracotta *Pietà* by Baccio from Montelupo, 1460-1535, and a *Charity*, a fresco by Ludovico Carracci) and the *Choir*, with its beautiful inlaid stalls made by fra Damiano Zambelli from Bergamo between 1528 and 1551, an authentic masterpiece combining artistic sensibility to expert craftmanship.

If we go back to the transept, by going down the right aisle, we come to the magnificent *Chapel of the Saint*, real devotional (and artistic) centre of the church.

The design of the chapel is by the architec Floriano Ambrosini (1597); the two large paintings at the sides of the stairs are by Lionello Spada (1576-1622), *The Fire Burns the Albigensian Books and Rejects the Bible of the Saint*; *The Saint Resurrects a Child* by Alessandro Tiarini (1577-1668). Further on we find the two grandiose and pathetic canvases of the *Resurrection of Napoleone Orsini after a fall from a horse* and the *Rescue of Some Ships* by Andrea Donducci called «Mastelletta» (1575-1665) who frescoed also the four *Patron Saints of the town* (Petronius, Proculus, Francis and Dominic) on the pendentives of the dome.

1. One of the magnificent, picture-quality, intarsia of the choir. 2. St. Dominic chapel: Guido Reni, the Glory of the Saint. 3. The chapel and ark of St. Dominic.

The radiant *Glory of the Saint* in the apse's basin is a masterpiece by Guido Reni (1575-1642) which can stand the comparison with the underlying *St. Dominic's Ark*, the beautiful and famous work whose elaboration took up five hundred years.

The altar frontal (*The Saint's Burial*) was carved in the workshop of Giovanni Battista Boudard in 1768; the altar foot with the *Epiphany and the Signs of Dominic's Sanctity* is by Alonso Lombardi (1532); the sarcophagus sculpted in the workshop of Nicola Pisano between 1265 and 1267 shows however the master's touch only on the front side, whose execution was later given to Lapo, while for the other sides the work was carried out by Arnolfo di Cambio with a small contribution by fra Guglielmo da Pisa.

The famous crowning was later added on, between 1469 and 1473, by Niccolò of Antonio, called «da Puglia» or «dell'Arca» for this splendid masterpiece of his. Around the highly elaborate spire he placed: below, the *Patron Saints of Bologna*; just over them, *Christ's Pietà and the Four Evangelists* dressed in Oriental robes and, on the top, the frowning *Eternal*

The magnificent ark, built in various stages between the 13th and the 18th centuries. 2. St. Dominic's ark: front of the sarcophagus and crowning. 3. St. Petronius, by Michael-angel.

3

77

1

5

ather. However, he left his work unfinished; in 475 the young Michaelangel was commissioned o sculpt three small statues: *St. Petronius* in the ront; *St. Proculus*, which resembles the David, n the back, and the *candlestick-holding Angel* n the right, which stands with its youthful trength and decision in contrast with the other ne by Niccolò, so beautiful but so delicate.

The *St. John the Baptist* on the back is by iirolamo Coltellini (1539-1545) and the precious *Reliquary* of the head is by Jacopo Roseto (1383).

The *Virtues* in the apse's niches are by Giovani Tedeschi (1651) while the lovely bust in white marble is a modern work representing the real ace of the Saint drawn from precise studies cared out on his skull by Prof. Fabio Frassetto.

Angel holding a candlestick, by Niccolò dell'Arca. 2. Anl holding a candlestick, by Michaelangel. 3. Back side of e sarcophagus and crowning. 4. St. Proculus, by Michaelgel. 5. Two Prophets, by Niccolò dell'Arca. 6. Jacopo Rose: reliquary with the head of St. Dominic (1383).

6

The cloister of the Deaths, dominated by the Saint's Chapel and the belltower. 2. St. Dominic Monastery: Inquisition hall. 3. The cell where St. Dominic died. 3

Via Farini

Via Farini resulted from the joining of four ancient streets made in 1860 after the annexion of Bologna to the Kingdom of Sardinia. It starts where via Dei Libri once was and, in order to recall the Law schools which had been located there since the 13th century, the Committee for an Artistic and Historical Bologna had a commemorative plaque placed in a pilaster of **Palazzo Cavazza** (n. 3), designed by Giuseppe Mengoni (1863).

Piazza Cavour, opened in 1867 and encircled by 19th-century buildings, such as **Palazzo Silvani** (n. 4) and the **Bank of Italy** (n. 6), whose arcades were decorated by Gaetano Lodi, looks onto via Farini.

Palazzo Guidotti (n. 9) is the result of readjustment works carried out by Coriolano Monti: the arcade on via Farini has still 11 capitals belonging to the older building.

After the 18th-century arcade of **Palazzo Pietramellara** (via Farini n. 14) we come to piazza Minghetti with the monument dedicated to the politician, by Giulio Monteverde, 1896, from which it is possible to reach the Medieval **Casa Caccianemici** (n. 11) located in via De' Toschi

1. Via Castiglione from north. 2. Minghetti Square with the monument of the politician (by Giulio Monteverde). 3. The adorned ceiling of the portico before the Bank of Italy. 4. Banking Palace Cassa di Risparmio, by Giuseppe Mengoni.

1

2

From 1868 to 1876 the **Palazzo della Cassa di** **isparmio** (Saving Bank's Palace) was built on a Farini (n. 22). It is the work of Giuseppe Men-ni, the architect who had designed also the Vit-rio Emanuele Gallery in Milan.

The Saving Bank also owns the Renaissance-yle **Casa Saraceni** building (n. 15) just in front, aracterized by a gracious tower, now made into roof terrace decorated with terracotta works.

The 19th-century street, which ends at the oss-roads with via Santo Stefano, fits right in th the town's older layout, thanks also to the tervention of Coriolano Monti from Perugia, ho designed a building (ns. 28-32) which could ct as a link between the old and new rows of ble palaces, without stressing the separation of e streets but instead creating a sort of second ain front corresponding to the Largo di Santo efano, besides the façade looking onto via arini.

3

Via dell'Archiginnasio

At the eastern limit of the historical section of the *Pavaglione*, where silk was once sold and bought (from the Latin *papilio*, butterfly, mediated through the French *papillon* or *pavillon*), often divided into the «inside Pavaglione», that is corte (yard) Galluzzi, and the «outside Pavaglione», today's piazza Galvani, we find the **Palazzo dell'Archiginnasio** with the 139 metres long *Portico del Pavaglione* underneath, which is the traditional and elegant walking mall of the town. Commissioned by Pope Pius IV Medici in 1561 as a unified and controllable seat for the town's Studium (University), it was erected in 1562-63 after a project by Antonio Morandi, also called Terribilia. The palace has only one floor over the portico with sandstone columns. Under the galleries of the beautiful square *courtyard* we find: on the ground floor, the *chapel of St. Mary of the Bulgarians* with fragments of frescoes by Bartolomeo Cesi and the altar-piece of the *Annunciated* by Calvaert; on the first floor, the *Anatomical Cabinet* built in pine and cedar wood by Antonio Levanti (1638-49), with linden wood statues by Silvestro Giannotti in the niches, and by Ercole Lelli (1735: the two *Skinned persons*) at the side of the chair. The chapel and the cabinet were destroyed by bombs on 29th January 1944, in an air-raid that razed the eastern wing of the palace, but were rebuilt in 1947-48. The restoration of the cabinet was terminated at the

1. *Archiginnasio, by Terribilia. 2. The courtyard with a two-tier open balcony. 3. Pavaglione arcade. 4. The Anatomical Theatre (17th century).*

1

nd of the 60's. On 18th April 1982 Pope John
Paul II went there to render visit to the old Studium. The building displays a peculiar and
unique heraldic decoration: thousands of painted and relief coats of arms from the 16th and
17th centuries, which recall the students elected
early to the posts of councillors, priors and rec-
tors within their respective «nations» and facul-
ties. The **Biblioteca Comunale dell'Archiginnasio** (the Archiginnasio Municipal Library) was
placed in the thirty lecture halls and in the two
assembly halls of the Law and Humanities students in 1838-39. This Municipal library which
is the largest of its kind in Italy was founded in
1801 and has grown in time thanks to many and
lavish grants, acquisitions and donations. It owns
about 600,000 volumes, 2,500 incunabula, 12,000
manuscripts, 15,000 books printed in the 16th
century, 10,000 engravings, 15,000 drawings. The
library has also a very important *Cabinet of
drawings and prints.*

*Open from Monday through Friday from 9 a.m. to
p.m. - Open on Saturdays from 9 a.m. to 1.30 p.m.*

---

*A «skinned person», by Ercole Lelli. 2. The desk of the
anatomical Theatre, with the two «skinned people». 3. Law
students' Main Lecture Hall, called Stabat Mater Room. 4.
Arts Students' Main Lecture Hall, now a reading room. 5.
A view of the upper open gallery.*

5

MUSEO CIVICO ARCHEOLOGICO

1

2

Beside St. Petronius's we find the Museo Civico Archeologico (the town's archeological museum) with its entrance at via dell'Archiginnasio n. 2. It was inaugurated on 25th September 1881 in the old palace of the Hospital of St. Mary of Death. The building, erected in the years 1336-39 and changed in 1565 by Antonio Morandi, also called Terribilia, through the addition of the arcade, was adapted to house a museum in 1878 following a design by Antonio Zannoni.

The museum was divided into different areas: the «Room of Antiquities» of the Institute of Sciences formed by the historical Aldrovandi Cospi and Marsili collections, which later became the «Antiquarian Museum of the University»; the «Comunitativo Museum» formed by the Municipal art collection to which the Pelagi collection was added in 1860 and which became the «Civic Museum» in 1871. The new Archeological Civic Museum (which had a Medieval section until 1962, now moved to Palazzo Ghisilardi Fava: see pag. 205), which in 1881 had already been endowed with the findings from the excavations carried out in 1871-81 in the necropoli of Villanova and Felsina, acquired later on the Capellini paleo-ethnological collection and the

5

ndings of the excavations carried out between
881 and 1924.

In the hall and in the courtyard (previously the
hurch and cloister of St. Mary of Death) we find
he valuable exhibition of *gravestones*; in the hall
here are also stones from the countryside and
mall urns from the ancient town, besides black
nd white mosaic floors from the town itself.
Among all these Roman remains we would like
o recall: the *Suarius Stela*, with a swine herder
nd 7 piglets; the *Stela of Q. Manilius Cordo*,
 pseudo-aedicule; the *Stela of the Togaed Man*,
rom Maccaretolo; the *limestone Sphynx*, from
orgo Panigale; the beautiful marble *loricaed
ust*, thought to be a statue of Nero (1st cent.
.D., originally from Piazza dei Celestini).

Also, we can admire two big *cylindrical Etrus-
an altars*, finely relief-decorated monoliths from
he 7th century B.C. which were found in 1985
 an ancient sacred ground in today's via Fon-
azza.

From the right end of the atrium one enters
he *Castt Gallery*: the collection of plaster casts

*and 2. Two views of the courtyard. 3. Room of the Felsina
ecropoles. 4. The Loricate, a Roman marble statue (1st cen-
ury). 5. The Maccaretolo Togate, a Roman statue and the
nerary stele of «Suarius». 6. Funerary stele of Cornelii (1st
entury B.C.).*

6

of the Civic Archeological Museum has been permanently set up in three rooms of the ex-hospital infirmary, and finally perform the educational purpose for which the collection was begun by the archeologist Edoardo Brizio in the late 1800's and continued by his successor Gherardo Ghirardini. The plaster casts were to serve as educational supports for University courses in Greek and Roman art history: those collected by Brizio and Ghirardini between 1877 and 1920 were added to a nucleus owned by the Palagi collection. The first room shows casts of works from the archaic period (600-480 B.C.) and the severe or Protoclassical period (480-350 B.C.), including the celebrated *Tyrannicides* and the *Discus thrower* by Myron. In the second room, casts of works from the Classical period (450-400 B.C.), including the *Spearman* by Polycletus, and from the second stage of the Classical period (400-323 B.C., including the superb *Hermes with the child Dionysius*, and finally from Hellenic period, whose sculptures here include the *Apoxiomenos* by Lisippo. The entrance to the room is dominated by effigy of *Athena Lemnia* by Phidias (450 B.C.), a reconstruction due to the great 19th century German archeologist Adolf Furtwängler, by joining the casts of the *Palagi Head* in this Museum and a torso kept in Dresden. The third room has casts of works from the Hellenic period, including the group of *Orestes and Electra*, and from the Roman period, including the winged *Brescia Victory* and other sculptures, mainly portraits.

From the first room, stairs (at the foot, a *marble bust of L.F. Marsigli* by Arturo Borghesani, late 1930's) leads to a hall with Gothic windows and other architectural remains of the Hospital of Death. Here the *Antiquities of Verucchio* (Rimini) from the 9th and 8th centuries B.C. are kept, deposited with the Superintendency for Antiques, Etruscan artifacts from digs carried out in 1893-94 and 1962-73.

In the courtyard, besides the numerous Classical, Greek, Roman and Christian inscriptions, we can see a beautiful *entablature* in Luni marble from Rodriguez palace; the series of *milestones* from *via Aemilia* are quite impressive: the highest one, 3.30 m, comes from areas around the Reno river and was dedicated to Augustus, the restorer of the street

The main collections of the Museum are on the first floor: Egyptian, Greek and Roman, Italian-Etruscan, Etruscan, archeological finds in the area of Bologna, the burial grounds of Villanova and the excavations of Antonio Zannoni, remains from Pre-Roman Bologna, from the Paleolithic and Iron Ages, and Celtic finds. Room I, Prehistory (manufacts found in the area of Bologna): to be noted *41 bronze axes* from Rocca di Badolo (show-case IV), *sandstone cast die for a sickle and two arrow-heads* from Priosta di Imola (show-case VII), *ossuaries* and *ashes urns* from the necropolis of Pragatto (show-

case IX), *finds from the «hut of the gold ornaments»* from Borgo Panigale, and *three zoomorphic figurines* (show-case XI). Room II, Prehistoric parallelisms.

Egyptian Antiquities (rooms III, IV, V). This collection, bought by Pelagio Palagi in 1831 from Giuseppe Nizzoli, the chancellor of the Austrian Consulate in Cairo, and donated by Palagi to the town in 1860, is the third in order of importance after Turin and Florence. In it we can admire all the classes of monuments, from amulets to scarabs (more than 2,000 pieces), to *shuebte* or burial statuettes (over 400 pieces), to mummies, painted sarcophagi, papyruses, funerary urns, to large and small stone and bronze statues to relief works and funerary stelae.

The so-called «New Kingdom» is particularly well documented. Room III: in the centre, *Portrait of King Amenhophis IV*, in black granite (18th dynasty); limestone *funerary stela* with relief works for the King Horemheb at Saqqara (19th dynasty, 1354-1346 B.C.); *wall panels from the tomb of Horemheb*, the general of Amenhophis IV (18th dynasty). Room IV: a black granite *statuette of a seated dignitary*, wearing a wig; it is the oldest piece in the Egyptian collection, and it dates back to the 4th dynasty (24th century B.C.); *statues of husband and wife* (the priest Amenhotep and his wife Merit, in limestone, 18th-19th dynasty); a rich collection of

3

huebte, of which we should mention the pieces from the tomb of the Pharaoh Sethi I (1318-1304 B.C.); the *Book of the dead* of the 19th dynasty; the marvellous *wooden statue of the naked girl*; the limestone *statue of the king's scribe Amenmes* offering the votive images of Osiris, Isis and Horus (19th dynasty); painted sarcophagi, painted boxes with the shape of mummies, mummies (a peculiar one is the *cat's mummy*), Room V: a granite *group of two statues of gods*, the vulture and the hawk (26th dynasty); the beautiful *Relief work of the King Nectanebo I* in black granite (30th dynasty); burial boxes, funerary stelae, votive relief works, amulets, scarabs, etc.

Greek Antiquities. Room VI: the magnificent *Palagi's Head*, or *Lemnian Athena*, Pentelic marble, a copy made at the time of Augustus from a 5th century B.C. bronze attributed to Phidias. In the show-cases: amphorae, one of

4

---

1. *Egyptian Antiquities: group of statues Amenhotep and Merit (XVIII-XIX dynasties). 2. Blue majolica shuebte of King Seti I. 3. Statue of Uahibra, black granite (XXVI dynasty). 4. Painted chest (XVIII dynasty). 5. Sarcophagus of the official Usai (XXVI dynasty).*

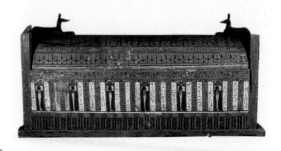

5

1

which is the *decorated amphora with handles shaped as ribbons*, an Attic ceramic work with black figures by the Greek Nikosthenes from the 6th cent. B.C.; oinochoe, craters, lekytoi or balm urns, skyphos, pelike, hydrias, kantaros. Among the kylikes (table vases) we would like to mention the world-famous *Codro's Cup*, from Vulci in Phidian style from the 5th century B.C.; there are also many clay statuettes, a precious group of *Tanagra* statuines, small bronzes, ceramics, votive reliefs, etc.

Roman Antiquities. Room IX: *cylindrical altar* in marble from Boncellino (Bagnacavallo) with pairs of cornucopias; *bronze trypod* from the last years of the Roman Empire; a marble *head of putto*; a nice *porphyry basin*; and also: small bronzes, ivories, pieces of roof tiles, amphorae, terracotta lamps, surgical instruments, scales, weapons, statues, capitals, metopes, terms, etc. Room VII: a *statue probably representing an Emperor*; a superb *bust from a Ionian statue*, perhaps a nude of an athlete, in marble from the 2nd century A.D.; a *bust of Aphrodite bathing*, a copy from the work of Doidalses of Bitinia (3rd century B.C.).

Italic-Etruscan Antiquites. Room VIII: two marvellous *alabaster urns* from Volterra (3rd cent. B.C.); Etruscan canopic vases, male and female terracotta heads, clay votive offerings, buccheri, painted Etruscan ceramics, tombs' furnishings; remains of the *choroplastic frieze of Civital-*

ba near Sassoferrato in the Marche (2nd century B.C.), with terracotta compositions representing Dionysus and Ariadne and the flight of the Gauls from Delphi; *urns from Chiusi* in relief terracotta.

Villanovan Antiquities, from the end of the 10th century to the first half of the 6th century B.C.. The Villanovan culture, on which the Etruscan colonization had good hold, takes its name from the excavation carried out at Villanova of Castenaso by Giovanni Gozzadini, after the discovery of the necropolis with 193 tombs in 1853. At that time the precious finds threw some light on the past of Bologna by allowing hypotheses on the Pre-Roman cultures around the town to be formulated. These hypotheses were later confirmed by the excavations carried out by Antonio Zannoni (necropolis of Certosa with 421 tombs from Felsina in 1869) and by the ones made by Gozzadini himself at Marzabotto besides those by Brizio and others. The findings fill the Rooms Xa, X and Xb, and they are so

1. Head of Lemnian Athena, a Greek copy from Fidias. 2. Apulian vase with volutes (4th century B.C.). 3. Villanova Benacci Askòs from the 8th century B.C. 4. Villanovan bi- conic ossuary with bowl (8th-9th centuries B.C.). 5. Array of a Villanovan tomb.

numerous that it is impossible to describe them here in this guide-book. We would like to mention the sandstone *Gozzadini Head* with a cubic structure (6th century B.C.); the famous *Benacci askos* in the shape of an animal, whose handles are two stylized horses, a terracotta work from the 7th century B.C.; the series of objects (14,841) found in 1877 by Zannoni in the «closet of St. Francis».

The Etruscan Civilization: this is Europe's most important Etruscan collection and it is exhibited in the large rooms X and XI. In this case, as well, it is impossible for us to give a detailed description of all the items. Room X: the *Arnoaldi Situla*, in the shape of a truncate cone (5th century B.C.); *head of kouros* (young man) in white marble from around 500 B.C., in deposit from the Marzabotto Museum; *small bronzes* from the votive drawer (ca. 480 B.C.) of the mountain shrine of Monte Acuto Ragazza; *small bronzes*, ca. 430 B.C., from Monte Capra. Among the many beautiful gravestone stelae, let us mention the *Big stela of the Giardini Margherita*, 5th century B.C., built for the deceased Vele Caicne. The famous *Situla of Certosa*, in the shape of a truncate cone, in bronze sheet, with four bands of relief figures (6th-5th centuries B.C.); the furnishings of the *Big Tomb* from the Giardini Margherita, the richest of the ones found in the Felsina's necropoles, with a *wood chest* measuring 3.5 m. x 2.5 m.; the furnishings of the *Tomb of*

1

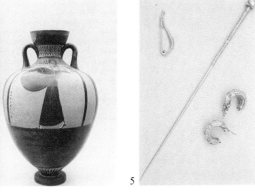

5

...he stool from the Giardini Margherita, 5th century B.C., in which a folding *ivory stool* is carved, the only example of such an object made from that material.

Roman and Gallic Civilizations. Room XII: ...he main aspects of the Gallic culture which graft-

. Etruscan bronze situla, from Certosa (5th century B.C.).
. Detail of Situla, with the train of spearbearers. 3.
...orseshoe-shaped Etruscan stele, from Certosa (4th centu-
...y B.C.). 4. Panathenaic amphora. 5. Buckles and pins of
...truscan make. 6. A devotee, small Etruscan bronze from
...lonte Acuto Ragazza (5th century B.C.).

6

ed on to the Etruscan civilization in the 6th century B.C. and in the 2nd century gave place to the Roman one are illustrated here together with specific characteristics of the Roman civilization typical of the Bologna's area. From the Gallic burial grounds: *two helmets* in bronze from the 3rd century B.C.; *gold diadem* with lanceolate leaves on oval gold sheets; a *bronze vase* in the shape of situla with modelled handle; a *oinochoe* with a three-lobed mouth and the handle shaped as a naked dancing boy; a *cap helmet* with gold embossed discs on the ear flaps; *iron sword* with bone hilt, 3rd century B.C.; candlesticks, mirrors, fibulae (bucles), armillae (armlets), shears, clay objects, andirons, bronzes, painted and unpainted ceramics. Roman antiquities: *Figure of a nymph lying on one side*, the decoration of a fountain from the 3rd century B.C.; *Cyma of a stela* with four portraits of men; *Relief* with scenes of gladiators from a sepulchral monuments; three *silver cups*, Roman-Hellenistic art; *clay bust* of running Eros. We can mention various objects in a show-case, such us a small bronze of *Barbarian horseman* from Claterna; a small bronze of *Diana* from Monteveglio; a terracotta *Eros* (1st century A.D.).

The Civic Archeological Museum is open from 9 a.m. to 2 p.m. from Tuesday through Saturday; on Sunday from 9 a.m. to 12.30 p.m. The museum is closed on Monday and on holidays falling during the week.

2

1. Bronze oinochoe (4th-3rd centuries B.C.). 2. Bronze helmet (4th-3rd centuries B.C.). 3. Gaul diadem in gold (4th-3rd centuries B.C.).

Between 1454 and 1502 the church was completely rebuilt and enlarged. The hospital, which was to be the forerunner of today's Ospedale Maggiore, was enlarged in 1518.

On 28th November 1668 one section of the church collapsed causing the death of eight people and the wounding of many others. Therefore, while the Hospital was transferred in via Riva Reno, where it remained till its distruction during the war on 24th July 1943, the Fellowship commissioned Architect Giovan Battista Bergonzoni to carry out the church's reconstruction, which he supervised until 1692 up to the cornice of the dome.

The dome was built in 1787 following a design by Architect Giuseppe Tubertini and became one of the most characteristic features of the Bologna's skyline. The façade was added in 1905.

The church's interior, on an elliptical plan, is very imposing; its decorations are very elegant, the figures of the four *Sibyls* on the pendentives are by Luigi Acquisti (1787).

The two larger side chapels are dedicated: to the *Blessed Riniero Fasani*, the founder of the Disciplinati movement, the left one where the

CHIESA DI S. MARIA DELLA VITA

(Via Clavature, 10). The origins of this church are strictly connected to the fate of the Disciplinati (or Battuti) movement, founded by fra Riniero Fasani in Perugia in 1260, which rapidly spread around Northern and Central Italy and came to Bologna soon after its inception. The first Disciplinati community of laymen to settle in town (they practised a strict discipline, publicly flogging themself in a show of penance, besides aiding poor pilgrims and the sick) founded here, next to the parish church of St. Vito (from which the name «da -near- St. Vito» came, later then changed into «della Vita» -of life-), a hospital and a chapel dedicated to the Virgin over which an oratory was built in 1435.

Church of S. Maria della Vita: the façade (1905). 5. Tubertini's dome marking the town's skyline.

5

97

painting by Domenico Pedrini (1728-1800) recalls an older painting by Cavedoni, kept in the oratory, and to the *Blessed Bonaparte Ghisilieri*, the first follower of Fasani in Bologna, the right one, in which he is buried and where the painting by Aureliano Milani (1675-1749) and the lively stucco putti by Angelo Piò (1690-1769) are to be found.

The lovely fresco representing the *Enthroned Virgin with Child* above the high-altar was perhaps painted by Simone dei Crocifissi (second half of the 14th century) on a side wall of the old church and was whitewashed in 1502. It was found by chance 1617 by a worker scraping the wall and soon became the centre of worship for the faithful.

In the right chapel of the high-altar there is the rightly famous terracotta *Pietà* modelled by Niccolò dell'Arca in 1463. It is considered one of the most original masterpieces of the Italian Quattrocento for its strong, vehement and expressive figures, and it still strongly affects the visitor although it has almost completely lost its former polychromy.

The sacristy was cut from a span of the older 15th-century church which had somehow survived the 17th-century renewal because the beautiful oratory, built between 1604 and 1617 by Bonifazio Socchi following a design by Floriano Ambrosini, still stands on it.

All the stucco works of the oratory are by Giulio Cesare Conventi (1577-1640) except for *St. Petronius* and *St. Proculus*, two early works by Alessandro Algardi (1598-1654); the massive group of the *Moving of the Virgin to her Sepulchre* is by Alfonso Lombardi (1522) and the painting over the altar (*Madonna with Child in Glory, the Blessed Riniero and Several Saints*) is by Giovanni Francesco Bezzi called «Nosadella» (ca. 1562).

The famous terracotta Pietà by Nicolò dell'Arca. 2. Pietà by Nicolò dell'Arca: detail with one of the Maries. 3. Pietà by Nicolò dell'Arca: detail with Christ and, from the left, Joseph of Arimathea, a Mary, the Virgin, and Mary Magdalene. 4. Oratory of S. Maria della Vita (detail): the Carrying of the Virgin, a terracotta work by Alfonso Lombardi.

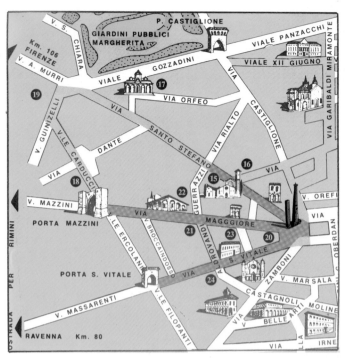

Via Santo Stefano

Via Santo Stefano is called after the group of churches known under the same name. The street starts at the right of the Mercanzia palace and ends at the gate making a notably varying urban layout; it is placed at times on different levels, a lower one for vehicular traffic and a raised one for pedestrian traffic. The latter level is often so large that it forms open spaces, used as squares by the people of Bologna.

Casa Alberici (n. 4), on whose 12th-century tower the room of a workshop was opened in 1273, which can still be seen today, stands next to **Case Seracchioli** (n. 2) which face Mercanzia square.

Casa de Bianchi (n. 14) offers in the inside quite a surprise: an Empire style grand staircase, decorated with stucco works by Bonaventura Furlani and statues by Domenico Palmerani.

Casa Bolognini (n. 18) from the 15th century has a peculiar cornice formed by fifty niches and small arches containing terracotta human heads and vases in classic shapes. The anthropomorphic theme is evokingly taken up again in the following century in another **Palace** (ns. 9-11) built again for the Bolognini family, so that both the palaces are benignly nicknamed «the palaces of the heads» according to popular tradition. The heads of the portico are really portrait-quality, each with varying physiognomy according to ancient standards, often sporting elaborate headdresses such as turbans or with well-groomed

beards or hair. They have been attributed to famous artists: Alfonso Lombardi and Nicolò da Volterra. The same device of heads seemingly stressing their neck on looking about, which can be verified by leaning on a column and looking up, is repeated on the second floor. The themes concocted for the capitals are no less refined: animal protomes, dolphins, rams, dragons and lions by Properzia de Rossi and Giacomo dalla Nave. By tradition the architectural structure is attributed to Formigine.

Another section of undoubted charm is the one of the **Case Beccadelli** (ns. 15-21) «grown» one next to the other between the end of the 15th century and the beginning of the 16th century: they have been badly touched up during the 18th century and the frescoes of Aspertini removed (at n. 15's). None the less they still are a unique example of how arcades in Bologna were used as viable means of linking up Gothic art themes with Renaissance ones.

1. *Via S. Stefano: Seracchioli Houses and the Alberici Tower (13th century). 2. Bolognini Palace (15th century). 3. Arcade of one of the Beccadelli Houses.*

3

101

BASILICA DI SANTO STEFANO

In 392, St. Ambrose, bishop of Milan, found here in the Jewish cemetery the relics of the Martyr Saints Vitale and Agricola from Bologna and placed them with their due honour in a small chapel. Half a century later, St. Petronius, bishop of Bologna, had a copy of the Holy Sepulchre in Jerusalem built next to that place of worship and in there he was later buried next to the empty sarcophagus representing the one of Christ.

In 727 the Langobards, after conquering the town, made the shrine their main religious centre in Bologna and, a few decades later, Charlemagne stopped here as a sign of devotion and took with him some relics for the Clermont Cathedral in France.

The shrine went through a period of neglect from which it came out thanks to the work of the Benedictine Brothers who took it over at the end of the 10th century and started a complete renewal and enlargement effort at the beginning of the 11th century, especially in the sections of the church dedicated to the Holy Land just at the time in which the Crusades were being launched.

From then on the basilica has come to us with its intricate maze of churches, courtyards, chapels, passageways, «renewed» and «restored» more than once, but none the less still laden with

1. Basilica of S. Stefano, or «Holy Jerusalem» compound
2. Church of the Crucifix, with an outer ambo and two sacophagi. 3. Crypt of the Abbot Martin.

describable fascination which is further increased by the many misteries placed between history and legend surrounding this church.

We can see facing the square on the left-hand side: the church of Saints Vitale and Agricola; the one of the Holy Sepulchre with a central plan; and finally, the one of the Crucifix with a round ambo, which was used to display the relics to the people, and two sarcophagi (in the right one the town's first bishops, such as Saints Zama and Faustinianus, had been buried).

An epigraphic dedication to the victorious Isis, belonging to a Roman temple which certainly stood nearby, is walled in the left side of this church. The marble slab was found in 1299 during excavation works in the square.

In the inside, which is the least preserved, we can see an expressive *Pietà* by Angelo Gabriello Piò (1690-1769), the elegant raised ark by Niccolò Aldrovandi (1438) and, in the presbytery restructured in 1637 according to a design by the architect Ottaviano Mascherino, two frescoes by Jacopo di Paolo, *Christ on the Road to the Calvary* and the *Crucifixion* (early 15th century). The crypt is quite outstanding: it was built in 1019 for the abbot Martino and one of its column marks the height of Jesus. This crypt is thought to be the first section of the group of churches rebuilt by the Benedictines in order to place there the relics of Saints Vitale and Agricola.

In the next church of the Sepulchre, there are seven marble columns belonging to the most ancient place of worship, probably dating back to the 5th century, while the rest date from the 12th century, the time of the reconstruction by the Benedictines.

The central aedicule represents Christ's Sepulchre and contains an urn with the relics of St. Petronius.

On both sides of the reliquary, two marble slabs decorated with elegant swags of leaves and flowers from a building dating back to Adrian's times (beginning of the 2nd century A.D.) separate two arks, one of which has been left empty to symbolize Christ's Sepulchre, and the other left for the burial of the bishop Petronius.

The reliefs (the *Three Maries at the Sepulchre*) date from the 14th century while the large symbols of the Evangelists on the pulpit date back to the 12th century. The capitals on the women's gallery are also quite interesting.

The next church of Saints Vitale and Agricola is probably the most evocative in the whole group of churches for its roughly-hewn elements, its many re-used ancient fragments (the really refined Ionian Capital from the 3rd century A.D. at bottom on the right), and the suffused half-darkness created by the alabaster-panelled windows. Along the left aisle, two small pits open on to fragments of an older mosaic flooring from the 6th century.

If we go back through the Sepulchre's church

2

and brush against the isolated column recalling
the flagellation's one, we then go out in the court
yard called «Pilate's» which was built, together
with the annexed small Trinity church, between
the 12th and 13th centuries by the Benedictine
in order to complete the project of reproducing
the places of worship in Jerusalem which held the
Holy Sepulcre.

The large stone basin in the centre, common
ly known as «Pilate's basin», was donated to the
church by the Lombard Kings Liutprando and
Ildebrando for the collection of the people
offerings, as can be seen in the inscription run
ning along its rim.

The big statue of *St. Peter* in the heavily re
stored Trinity church is a fake from the last cen
tury; whereas the *Nativity* scene of gilded and
painted wood, made in the workshop of Simon
dei Crocifissi at the end of the 14th century,
of superb quality.

From here we can go directly to the nearby
Benedictine cloister whose lower tier was built be
tween the 10th and the 11th centuries, while the
upper one, more ornate and elegant, was added
in the 13th century. In the latter, the side toward
the church is quite interesting especially for its
imaginative capitals some of which are anthropo
morphic.

The central well-curb dates back to 1632; in
1925 the «*Lapidarium*», set up as a memento for
the citizens of Bologna fallen during World War

4

. The inside of St. Sepulchre's church. 2. St. Sepulchre's ae-icule (12th-13th centuries). 3. The inside of Saints Vitale and Agricola's church. 4. Roman capital used in the building (3rd century).

2

Holy Trinity church, the inside. 2. Nativity scene by Si-
*one dei Crocifissi, polychrome wood sculpture from the 14th
*ntury. 3. Pilate's basin placed at the centre of Pilate's court-
*rd. 4. The magnificent cloister with two-tiered open galleries
*0th-13th centuries). 5. Stone well with ring and delta from
*32. 6. Romanesque steeple, in common to all the «seven
*urches».

6

I (1915-1918), was placed along the walls of th lower tier.

From the cloister we can move on to the ol chapter hall and to the small but quite interest ing museum of the basilica, which exhibits, be sides many other items: on the right room, th outstanding *sarcophagus* (just recently restored of *St. Agricola* (late 11th century) and a preciou collection of 14th-century paintings, amon which let us recall a large polyptych with th *Saints Mark, John, James and Anthony Abbo* signed by Giovanni Ottonello and a tryptych wit the *Saints Benedict, Sistus and Proculus* by S mone dei Crocifissi; the touching canvas by Tiari ni (1577-1668), representing St. Martin raising th widow's son from the death, is also quite beau tiful; in the *Chapel of the Bandage*, a finel evocative architecture from the end of the 16t century (Benda), we can admire a *Slaughter o the Innocents* attributed to Marco Berlinghie from Lucca (ca. 1255), the only remaining fres co of the ones decorating the Holy Sepulchre' church; *St. Petronius* by Giovanni di Balducci from Pisa (first half of the 14th century); the o nate wooden *sarcophagus of the 40 Martyrs* b Gaspare and Antonio Billi (1568) and the pre cious *reliquaries* of St. Petronius (by Jacop Roseto, 1380), St. Florianus (the cell is from 145 and the foot from 1526) and of the Bandage (16t century).

2

*The old Chapterhouse Hall houses now the Basilica's muse-
m. 2. Alessandro Tiarini: St. Martin raises the widow's son
om death. 3. Simone dei Crocefissi: triptych with the saints
bbot Benedict, Pope Sistus and martyr Proculus. 4. Mar-
Berlinghieri: the Slaughter of the Innocents, detail (13th
ntury).*

4

CHIESA DI S. GIOVANNI IN MONTE

The origins of this church are closely linked to the one of S. Stefano. The spurious «Life of St. Petronius», written by a Benedictine monk from S. Stefano's in the 12th century, narrates that not far from the building reproducing the Holy Sepulchre the Bishop Saint (5th century) had a round pavillion, similar to the one erected in Jerusalem on the way up to the Mount of Olives, built on this small hill. The toponym of «Mount Oliveto» was already used in 1017 in documents from Bologna and the remains of a round building are to be found under the floor of today's church, by the small central altar.

In 1118 the small church went to a Canons' community that commissioned the building of a new crossed-planned church in the 13th century, further enlarged according to the Gothic style between 1440 and 1450.

The extraordinary artistic wealth of the church was heavily depleated by the sales made in the 18th century and the pillage carried out by Napoleon's troops: paintings by Raphael, Perugino, Ercole Roberti, Cima da Conegliano and others were taken away from the church. However, what is left is still invaluable.

The brickwork façade, with a curvilinear crowning (1474) of Venetian taste, has a fierce-looking *Eagle*, the symbol of St. John the Evangelist, by Niccolò dell'Arca (ca. 1481) over the portal.

The three stained-glass windows, the *En-*

throned Virgin with Child, St. John at Patmos the coat of arms of the client Gabione Gozzadini, were made between 1467 and 1482 by the master glass-maker Cabrini from a design of Francesco del Cossa.

In the second chapel on the left, the three paintings by Guercino, *St. Francis Praying, St Jerome* and *St. Mary Magdalene* (1645) are the first works commissioned to the painter in Bologna by a public client. The last chapel to the left (Architect Arduino Arriguzzi, 1514) was commissioned by the Blessed Elena Duglioli dall'Olio who is buried here, and who called Raphael to paint expressly for it his famous canvas *St Cecilia*. Now, in the frame by Formigine there is a 19th-century copy by Clemente Albéri.

In the main chapel, the altar-piece, the *Crowned Madonna among Christ, the Eternal Father and six Saints*, is by Lorenzo Costa (1501), the valuable *Crucifix* on panel is by Jacopino dei Bavosi, a lively painter active in Bologna from 1350 to 1380, and the wonderful *choir stalls* were inlaid by Paolo Sacca from Cremona between 1523 and 1527. The sacristy with its 16th-century furniture and an inlaid wood lectern from 1720 is quite interesting.

If we go down along the right aisle, at the third altar we come across a mature work by Lorenzo Costa (1497), an *Enthroned Madonna and Saints*.

The stone column with a big Romanesque cross at the centre of the nave dates back to 801 and replaces an even older one: it represents the only remain of the round pavillion from Petronius's times. The small altar is from the 11th century while the wonderful *Christ at the Column*, in wood, seems to be the work of an unknown 16th-century sculptor from Pavia.

After crossing the up-hill street that leads to S. Giovanni in Monte, and having passed by some modern buildings, erected after World War II on the rubbles made by air-raids which destroyed also the Teatro (theatre) del Corso, inaugurated in 1805 at the time of Napoleon's visit, we come to the Neoclassical façade of the former **Albergo del Corso** (Promenade Hotel) (n. 37) in which the poet Giacomo Leopardi once stayed.

Palazzo Vizzani (n. 43), which was started in 1559 and stands at a higher level than the street, has a Mannerist façade marked in its horizontal bands by projecting string-courses; in the strongly assertive architectural layout, perhaps carried out by Bartolomeo Triachini, the Doric columns and the caryatids are placed under the running architrave and the windows' gables respectively. Inside the palace there are still many important frescoes: the *Blinding of Polyphemus* by Pellegrino Tibaldi, *Tales of Cyrus* and *Allegories of Glory and Fame* by Lorenzo Sabbatini, and 19th-century decorations by Antonio Basoli and Felice Giani.

Palazzo Zani (n. 56), which dates also back to the 16th century, is by Floriano Ambrosini and is now the seat of the Consortium for Land Reclamation in the Reno Valley. In a vault on the ceiling in the «piano nobile» we can admire a fresco by Guido Reni, the *Fall of Faethon*, and the perspective quadratura paintings by Agostino Mitelli and Angelo Michele Colonna. The noble abodes of strada Santo Stefano (St. Stephen's street) hide inside precious works of art: for example, the grand staircases of **Palazzo Pallavicini** (n. 45), **Palazzo Varrini** (n. 57) and **Palazzo**

3

de Bianchi (n. 71); this one is a masterpiece by Antonio Ambrosi (1770) who applied in it the elements of a selectively refined aesthetic sense.

The showy taste of the 18th century is to be found in the façade (1752) of **Palazzo Agucchi** (n. 75) by Carlo Francesco Dotti, where the «piano nobile» is evidentiated by a series of small balconies terminating in the strongly projecting central balustrade. In the 18th century Bologna went through a great surge of new private dwellings all vying with each others in elegance and style, which caused many family coffers to be completed squandered. The arcade is used again as the unifying element of the street by harmonizing adjacent buildings from different centuries. It is also a structure to be used by the community at large, to be enjoyed at a slower walking pace, to foster contacts and communication among people.

With the **Conservatorio del Baraccano** (n. 119) we come to a public building complex, because it was used in the Renaissance as a charitable institution. The building of the arcade, just after 1491, evidentiates the charitable function of this structure, the will to renew and embellish the town by inserting multiple-purpose architectural patterns such as this one, to be used as a passageway and a building. The passer-by is almost taken aback by the discovery of capitals with ever-changing decorative motifs: leaves, shells, putti in an amazing explosion of invention and creativity for each span. In 1528 the building, which today houses the district's community centre, was transformed into a boarding school for poor girls. From its scenic large vault it is possible to have a general view of the church of the Madonna del Baraccano.

Church of S. Giovanni in Monte: the 1474 façade. 2. St. John's eagle, a magnificent terracotta work by Nicolò dell'Arca. 3. Via S. Stefano: Vizzani Palace (16th century).

Chiesa di S. Maria del Baraccano. A small chapel was raised here in 1403 in order to protect an image of the *Virgin with Child* which had been painted maybe by Lippo di Dalmasio (late 14th century) inside the town walls' baraccano or barbacane (barbican - defence tower) which can still be seen behind the church.

In 1472 Giovanni II Bentivoglio, Lord of the town, had the ancient image touched up and enlarged by the talented painter Francesco del Cossa from Ferrara who was commissioned also to add the portraits of the Bentivogli's ancestor, Giovanni I, and of Maria Vinciguerra who had fostered the worship of the image.

In 1512, after the aborted attempt to blow up the barbican with a bomb by Peter of Navarre, who had laid siege to the town at the orders of Consalvo of Cordoba, the decision to enlarge the chapel and build the church as we see it now, with the later (1524) addition of a large portico, was taken and the works began.

Architect Agostino Barelli designed the dome, added on in 1682. Inside, on the left altar, the *Contest of St. Catherine of Alexandria* is by Prospero Fontana (1512-1597).

The main chapel has many valuable marble decorations made by Lorenzo Bargellese following a design by Architect Arduino Arriguzzi in 1512, surrounding the above-mentioned image of Mary by Cossa and also in the gorgeous entrance archway.

The lateral statues of *St. Rocco* and *St. Sebastian* have been doubtfully attributed to Alfonso Lombardi (1497-1537); even though more recently, after the restoration of St. Sebastian, the name of Donatello has been made as the author of the statue the attribution seems quite far-fetched. The Baroque decorations date back to 1767.

According to a centuries-old tradition, newly married couples come here, after the wedding ceremony, to «receive the Peace».

On the side altar the *Procession of St. Gregory Magnus* was painted by Cesare Aretusi around 1580 from a design by Federico Zuccari.

The openly scenic large vault framing the church on via S. Stefano was raised by Architect Giuseppe Jarmorini in 1779 by enlarging the previous similar structure from 1497.

---

1. Church of S. Maria del Baraccano: the 1682 dome crowns the 16th-century place of worship. 2. Giosuè Carducci's house, once S. Maria del Piombo church. 3. Tosti: the Poet's marble bust.

112

The street ends with the **Barriera di Santo
efano** (St. Stephen's barrier), or Gregorian one,
e old customs' office (1843), formed by two
mmetrical buildings, designed by Filippo An-
lini, which replaced the 13th-century Medieval
te razed a few years earlier.

USEO E BIBLIOTECA
ARDUCCI -
USEO DEL RISORGIMENTO

In piazza Carducci n. 5, the **House of Giosuè
arducci** stands against the remains of the third
nd the last to be built) town' walls. It is charac-
rized by church-like features. In fact it is one
 twelve shrines built by the people of Bologna
the town borders. It was erected in 1502-1503
order to place there the bas-relief image of *Pie-
*, made on metal, perhaps lead, and for this rea-
n it came to be known as *St. Mary of the Pie-
 or *St. Mary of the Lead*. The arcade with its
upled columns dating back to 1598 was remade
1611 and in 1653. In 1798 the church was sup-
essed and in 1801 it became a private dwelling.
e arcade was walled in 1871. Carducci went
 live there on 8th March 1890 and died there
 16th February 1907. In 1902 Queen Margheri-

3

113

with a section on Italian literature. Among th many mementoes of Carducci let us recall the fo lowing: the *parchment and the medal of th Nobel Prize* (1906); the poet's *University rob* his *gypsum death mask* made by Golfarelli on th next morning after his death; *autographs* by Ma zini, Garibaldi, Cairoli and other patriots. The are also many portraits of Carducci: bronze bus by E. O. Rosales and Adriano Cecioni; paintin by Augusto Majani and Vittorio Corcos; a ma ble bust by Tosti.

When the restoration is completed, Casa Carduc (tel. n.347952) can be visited from 9 to 12 a.m. a from 3 to 5 p.m. during the week and on Sunday fro 9 to 12 a.m.: groups of no more than 5 people at time are admitted for the visit always guided by t. Museum's keeper.

ta had bought all his books and in 1906 the whole building. At the death of the poet she bequeathed the house and the library to the Municipality of Bologna on condition that it was to be preserved and upkept in its original state. Extensive resto- ration works carried out in 1986-88 have unco- vered the area set originally as a church on the ground floor and strengthened the building's structure. The poet's apartment is on the first floor: an evocative 19th-century home with every- thing to make life in it quite enjoyable (furniture, furnishings, knick-knacks, etc.). Everything is as it was left on 16th February 1907: the rooms and the furnishings form the Carducci Museum and Library. The poet's library includes 40,000 books, 11 incunabula, 94 albums of autographs, 208 volumes of manuscripts, 35,437 letters to Carducci and also a section on the literary production of Carducci and on him, together

1. The Library in Carducci's house. 2. The University r of Carducci. 3. The parlour of Carducci's house. 4. Ris gimento Museum. Carlo Ademollo: Ugo Bassi in the pri of Comacchio. 5. Helmet of the Civil Guard and shawl w Pope Pius IX and the «Edict of Forgiveness». 6. Anto Muzzi: Chase of the Austrians out of Porta Galliera.

Since 1991 the ground floor holds the *Civic Risorgimento Museum*, created in 1893 and hosted until 1990 with the Civic Archeological Museum in the-Hospital of Death. The display room is the old ecclesiastic room, with three small naves, of S. Maria del Piombo, freed from the apartments into which it had been divided. The restored frescos on the vaults are from the 17th century. In the adjacent rooms, once the sacristy, are a room for temporary exhibits, the management offices and a classroom. Within the framework of a cultural project directed by Prof. Angelo Varni - which includes events of the Risorgimento within the broader history of Bologna from the Napoleonic period to World War - the Museum is divided according to topic: secret societies, 1848 in Bologna, the unification of Italy, firearms. Considerable materiale is on display, including some very famous paintings (such as *Ugo Bassi in the Comacchio prison*, by Carlo Ademollo; *The Austrians driven out from Porta Galliera*, by Francesco Zauli Sajani, etc.), and «curiosities» such as the bronze mitre and staff which served in the late 18th century to disguise the statue of Gregory XIII in Piazza Maggiore as St. Petronius, and the «first stone» of

4

5

a Column of Peace which was to be built in Piazza Galvani.

The Risorgimento Museum (tel.. 347592) may be visited on weekdays from 9 a.m. to 1 p.m., Sundays from 9 a.m. to 12:30 p.m.. Closed Mondays and holidays.

Next to the House, on the embankment of the old town's walls, the **Monument to Giosuè Carducci**, a complex composition in Carrara marble by Leonardo Bistolfi lies within a verdant garden. This apotheosis Art Nouveau sculpture was designed and carved in 1918 and inaugurated by the King and Queen of Italy in June 1928.

At the centre the *Poet's pensive figure* dominates the composition having as a background a *triptych* (12 m. long and 2.60 m. high) divided by pilaster-strips and cariatyds, with symbolic representations of the poet's early works, from the «Barbarian Odes» to the «Motherland's Song». On the left we can see the *Group of Nature*, on the right the animated *Group of Freedom* (the «sauro destrier della canzone» - the sorrel steed of the song). The vast massive sculpture was restored at the beginning of the 80's.

6

Basilica di S. Antonio di Padova (via Jacopo della Lana, 2). Built in Neo-Gothic style by Architect Carlo Barberi and terminated in 1903, this church is decorated with mural paintings by Giacomo Gemmi who made them between 1906 and 1911. The two chapels at the side of the main one contain also mural paintings by father Eusebio Gelati (the *Eucharisty's Institution*) and by father Augusto Centofanti (*Tales of St. Francis*) made

around 1914. The steeple dates from 1928.

The church, however, is known more for the Antoniano activities carried out by the small Franciscan community which is particularly active in welfare, social work and cultural activities. Its «Piccolo coro» (small choir), formed by children, is quite well known throughout the world, and its activities for children are widespread but its highlight is the «Zecchino d'oro» competition (Gold sequin). The art exhibitions and the poor people's kitchen are also to be remembered and the latter has inspired the painter Lorenzo Ceregato to make his large-scoped fresco *The Hymn to Bread* in 1983.

1. Pistols and medals of Murat, according to the «Proclame of Rimini» (1815). 2. Busby and officer's uniform of the hussars (1848). 3. Fontana: The movement of Savigno in 1834. 4. Leonardi Bistolfi, Monument to Giosuè Carducci (1910-28). 5. The figure of the Poet, deep in thought. 6. The Neo Gothic Basilica of St. Anthony of Padua.

117

The first layout of Strada Maggiore as a road can be traced back ideally to the Roman Aemilian Way, which was connected by a large obtuse angle to the decumanus maximum, today's via Ugo Bassi and Rizzoli, thus providing a link between the town's central areas and the outer ones destined for residential dwellings and production activities or for burial grounds, as was the case for the ancient Villanovan cemeteries.

BASILICA DEI SANTI BARTOLOMEO E GAETANO

Already in the 11th century a small church had stood here (n. 5) over a crypt whose building had been attributed to St. Petronius although there are no written document attesting to it. In 1209 the church was gutted by fire but was soon to be rebuilt because we know that in 1253 a cloister, in which at least since 1288 a monastery of Cluniac nuns had been housed, was built next to the church.

In 1516, however, the church dedicated to St. Bartholomew and the monastery were razed on an order of the church's prior, the apostolic protonotary Giovanni Gozzadini who had wanted to enlarge the building and to include the prior's palace in it as well.

The commission was given to Andrea Formigine who raised the magnificent arcade deco-

rated with sandstone fretwork (unfortunally it is now quite damaged) in whose execution Francesco da Como, Giovanni Andrea de' Zardi and others also participated. In 1517 the works were suddenly stopped with the assassination of Gozzadini and they were taken up again only in 1599 when the place of worship passed in the hands of the Teatini, an order of regular monks founded in 1524 by St. Gaetano from Thiene in the

1

wn of Chieti (Teatino means a person who lives
Chieti or was born there).

Within the enclosure of the arcade the Teatini
d the new church built according to the design
Architect Giovan Battista Natali therefore ad-
ng to the old dedication to St. Bartholomew
e one to their founder.

The building of the church, in which the ar-
itect Agostino Barelli participated by adding
me variations, ended with the raising of the
me and the elegant steeple between 1688 and
94 (only the steeple's spire dates from 1748).
e side door at the head of the arcade is very
pressive (16th century).

The inside is very sumptuous.

Angelo Michele Colonna and Giacomo Al-
resi frescoed the nave (*The Glory of St. Bar-
olomew* - 1667) while the brothers Antonio
useppe Rolli decorated the dome and its vault
591).

The *St. Anthony from Padua* on the second
ar to the left is by Alessandro Tiarini
577-1668) and on the third one we can see the
steries of the rosary made by Domenico Ma-
Canuti (1620-1684).

The famous oval-shaped *Virgin with the Sleep-
; Child*, characterized by an incredible feeling
tenderness, on the transept's altar is a master-
ce by Guido Reni who put in it a deep reli-
us sentiment (1575-1642).

Behind the massive high altar, designed by
olo Canali (1618-1680), the three large scenes
rrating the *Martyrdom* and the *Miracles of St.
rtholomew* were painted by Antonio Fran-
schini and Luigi Quaini in 1693 with the help
the ornamentalist Enrico Haffner.

If we go down the right aisle we can see four
ars: in the first one, three paintings, the *Dream
St. Joseph*, the famous *Annunciation* called
the «beautiful angel», and the *Birth of Jesus*
de by Francesco Albani in 1633; in the second
e, the fanciful wall decorations by Angelo
chele Colonna (1600-1687), who was the
patron of the chapel, around the *St. Andrea
ellino* by Lorenzo Garbieri (1580-1654); in the
rd, the *St. Charles Kneeling in front of the
rallo Sepulchre*, quite ruined by humidity,
inted in 1614 by Ludovico Carracci.

The outside chapel, which is the church's bap-
try, was decorated according to the design of
oardo Collamarini (1864-1928). It contains an
l image of the *Virgin with Child* which had
ginally been painted on the outer wall of the
risenda tower and removed from there in 1871
en the oratory which protected it was des-
yed.

Basilica of the Saints Bartholomew and Gaetano near the
o Towers (17th-18th centuries). 2. Strada Maggiore, from
east. 3. The 16th-century arcade of S. Bartholomew's by
migine. 4. Strada Maggiore: Borghi Mamo House (14th
tury).*

The restoration works in **Palazzo Lupari** (n.
11) have brought to light the paving of the Roman road which has been left uncovered inside
the building so as to make it possible for the people to see it.

Casa Bonvalori (n. 13), restored in 1907 under the auspices of the Committee for Historical
and Artistic Bologna, which had the old, ruined
by time, ferrules and two-light windows replaced
or fixed, is an example of late-Gothic private architecture.

Casa Sorgi (ns. 15-17) was the first house to
be built with bricks in 1121, when in Bologna private buildings were still made with the wood cut
in the forests which surrounded the town.

Palazzo Gessi (n. 20): on the front, built in
1580, we can see the coat of arms of Gregory
XIII, the Pope with whom the Gessi family was
related.

Palazzo Fantuzzi (n. 22) offers an example of
a 16th-century front raised on a 15th-century arcade; the staircase, rebuilt in 1750 by Giovanni
Carlo Bibiena, is decorated with statues by Filippo Scandellari.

Casa Sampieri (n. 24) is decorated with frescoes by Carracci, which, in three rooms, narrate
episodes of the life of Hercules; the ceiling of
another room was painted by Guercino.

An arcade with rows of pilasters (n. 26), covered with an even ashlar-work, mark the Neo-

4

Classic taste which architect Santini applied for the house of the musician Gioacchino Rossini. It is possible to see an architectural example from the 13th century in **Casa Isolani** (n. 19): nine-metres high oak beams are embedded over plaster bases.

Palazzo Riario (n. 34), built in the mid 16th century, was restructured in 1798 by Giovan Battista Martinetti who kept intact the decorative frieze inspired by the decorations of the Roman temple of Antoninus and Faustina which are reproduced in three other spans of the arcade. Inside there are still rooms with their original 19th-century paintings: a room with forest scenes by Vincenzo Martinelli, frescoes by Pietro Fancelli in the Astronomy Room and a tempera landscape by Luigi Busatti in the courtyard.

Among the reconstructed buildings of the late 18th century it is possible to see a «tuata or tubata», that is a tower, commonly known as the **Torre degli Oseletti** (between n. 34 and n. 36). This nice looking defensive building raises over an escarp base, which had been previously buried and was brought to light in 1924 during restauration works which, however, reduced the thickness of the selenite ashlar cover by bringing it too close to the edge of the adjacent arcade. The tower is hidden up to the height of the palace front but soars over it among the roof-tops.

Palazzo Bonfioli (n. 29), which now houses the Institute of German Culture, still has a fanciful

spiral staircase decorated with stucco statues an painted motifs of flowers and greenery. The decoration of the friezes on the «piano nobile», inspire by the history of the Roman Republic, was con missioned to a team of fresco painters, Lionel Spada, Lucio Massari and Francesco Brizio. I stead the frescoes on the first courtyard and on th small covered balcony, dedicated to the epic poer Gerusalemme Liberata (The Liberation of Jerus lem), have been completely lost.

Palazzo Tartagni (n. 42) still displays in its a cade the 15th-century terracotta mascarons an in the inside the frescoes by Petronio and Pietr Fancelli.

1. Gioannetti house (15th century). 2. Isolani house (13th ce tury). 3. Davia Bargellini Palace (17th century). 3. The «Λ lantes' portal» viewed from the airy arcade of the church Servi.

PALAZZO DAVIA BARGELLINI

The grand home of Camillo Bargellini, without an arcade, as was often the custom for senatorial palaces, stands in strada Maggiore 44: the clear and pure façade, counterpointed by the cornices and the windows' jutting tympana, is characterized by a large portal - the only one of this genre in Bologna - flanked at each side by two telamones, which have contributed to the popular name of «palace of the giants» given to this building. Planned by Bartolomeo Provaglia in 1638 and built in about twenty years by the master builder Antonio Uri, Palazzo Davia Bargellini came into the hands of Virgilio Davia in 1839 and in 1876 to the Davia Bargellini Charitable Institution, established by Giuseppe Davia. The plasticly modelled telamones, or atlantes, in «masegna» stone from the Appennines ranges near Bologna, were sculpted by Gabriello Brunelli (the right one) and Francesco Agnesini (the left one) and put in place in 1658. The open grand staircase from 1730, decorated with stucco works by Giuseppe Borelli, is the result of the elaboration of different projects made by Torreggiani, Dotti, and Conti. The **Civico Museo d'arte industriale** and the **Galleria Davia Bargellini** (the Civic

4

Museum of Industrial Art and the Davia Bargellini Gallery) have been housed on the ground floor of the palace since 1924. In their layout, the seven rooms of the exhibition still reflect to a large extent the concepts on what a museum should be and offer which have inspired the museum's first curator, Francesco Malaguzzi Valeri, then supervisor of art galleries. The items of the Museum of Industrial Art are exhibited without any attempt to display them systematically preferring a more evocative outlook; the paintings, which demonstrate in their high-quality level the extent and variety of a single family's high art patronage, belong almost all to the Charitable Institution. Extensive restoration works were carried out in the Museum under the auspices of the Municipality in the years 1983-1984. The items on exhibit are more than one thousand. Room 1, furniture and rustic objects from Bologna from the 16th-17th centuries; of particular interest are the *scales* of the local Mint (from 1685 and 1786) and the collection of *albarelli* and other vases originally belonging to the «della Vita e della Morte» (of Life and Death) apothecary shops. Room 2, Renaissance furniture: a *bust of Gaspare Bargellini*, a terracotta work by Vincenzo Onofri; a *Virgin with Child*, also called *The Virgin of the Teeth*, a beautiful panel by Vitale da Bologna from 1345; the *Pietà*, a tempera work on a panel by Simone dei Crocefissi, 1368; *Virgin with Child*, a 15th-century panel, an early masterpiece by Bartolomeo Vivarini; four *woodden automata* from 1451, previously in the clocks' exhibition in the Municipal Palace; the *Mystical marriage of St. Catherine* by Innocenzo da Imola. The carved walnut *wedding chest* from the 16th-century school of Formigine is exquisite. Room 3: devotional object from the 17th and 18th centuries: in the room, set up as a noble family's chapel, there are sacred vessels and vestments, paintings

and sculptures. Let us mention a *Crucifix* by Alessandro Algardi; the fine *Virgin with Child*, a polychromatic terracotta work by the school of Giuseppe Mazza. Room 4, middle-class 17th- and 18th-century furniture, furnishings, an important collection of terracotta sculptures: *Two Peasants*, and *Two Shepherds* by Angelo Piò; *Madonna, Fortitude, Apollo, Two Female Figures, Magdalene's Communion*: these are some of the works by Giuseppe Mazza to be found in this exhibition; among the many paintings, let us recall the *Crucifixion* by Calvaert and *Sisara's Death* by Franceschini. Room 5, magnificent Baroque furniture from the 17th and 18th centuries, as the *architectural chest of drawers* topped by a cabinet from the 16th centuries; the famous canvas with the three *Dice Players* by Giuseppe M. Crespi; the *Deposition* by Giuseppe M. Crespi; the *Carrier* and the *Hunter* by Luigi Crespi; a *Landscape* by Paul Brill; *Head of an Old Man* by Simone Cantarini; two *Portraits of a Man* by Domenico M. Canuti; *St.*

1. Davia Bargellini Museum: the 18th-century ceremonial sedan. 2. Two farmers, terracotta figurines for a Nativity scene by A. Piò (18th century). 3. Puppet theatre (18th century). 4. Giuseppe M. Crespi: Dice players.

2

ancis of Assisi by Mastelletta. Room 6, carved
d gilded 17th- and 18th-century furniture: ta-
es, easy-chairs, candelabra, ceremonial folding
airs, frames; an exquisite *ceremonial sedan-
air* in black painted wood from the 18th cen-
ry; an interesting *18th-century a villa*, a
production in a very small scale and really
tailed. The following works hang on the walls:
veral paintings by Franceschini, Mirandolese
d Bigari; *St. John the Baptist* by Mastelletta,
ucifix with the Virgin and Saints by Guido
eni, *Portrait of a Lady* by Luigi Crespi, *Por-
it of a Bargellini Child* by Felice Torelli. Room
window display objects, ceramics, terracotta
ms: ceramics of Bologna and Emilia from the
nes of the Bentivoglio family to the end of the
th century, Wedgwood, Saxonia, Capodimon-
and Old Ginori porcelain, Murano glass; fig-
ines of the nativity scene by Piò, Mazza and
Maria; embroideries from the 18th century;
ascinating *puppet theatre* originally belonging
the Albicini from Forlì and decorated with
mpera painted scenes inspired by the Bibiena
mily, and 32 gorgeously dressed puppets, tes-
ying to the theatrical taste common even in the
mily life of the Baroque *élites*.

*he exhibit at Palazzo Davia Bargellini can be visited from
.m. to 2 p.m. from Tuesday to Saturday; on Sunday from
.m. to 12.30 p.m.; the museum is closed on Mondays and
ring holidays falling within the week.*

4

1

BASILICA DI S. MARIA DEI SERVI

Among the great mendicant orders which were founded in the 13th century the Serviti were the third in order of time, after the Franciscans (1211-13) and the Dominicans (1218), to settle within the walls of Bologna (1261). In 1346 they had started the building of their church here, and already in 1386 Brother Andrea Manfredi from Faenza, the Order's General, commissioned the enlargement of the church, which he had also designed, to Antonio di Vincenzo, the same architect who was going to start the building of the huge St. Petronius's church four years later.

The church's construction went on at an extremely slow pace: in 1437 the apse of the main chapel was terminated, in 1470 the ambulatory with three radiating chapels was added and only in 1504 were the ribbed vaults of the nave terminated. The arcade that in its older section runs along the church's side and which was built by Antonio di Vincenzo in 1393 is extremely graceful and charming. Three more spans towards Maggiore (Main) Gate were added to the older section in 1492, and in 1521 a new wing of the arcade was added to the church's façade. The ingenious quadrangular arcade along via Guerrazzi was ended in 1852-1855 in accordance to the older lines.

The inside of the church, with three naves, is characterized by harmonious and well-balanced Gothic lines.

The altars set against the lateral walls between the 16th and the 18th centuries have greatly increased the church's artistic wealth but, by blocking the side windows, they have darkened the inside while enhancing the great flow of light coming through the apse.

On the first altar on the left, inside an elegant Baroque niche (by the architect Francesco Tadolini) we can admire the nice *Our Lady of Sorrows* by Angelo Gabriello Piò (1690-1769); on the second one, the *Noli Me Tangere*, canvas painted with a refreshingly graceful classical style by Francesco Albani in 1664 when he was already sixty-six years old.

Above the side entrance, we can see the massive tomb of Lodovico Gozzadini (died in 1536),

a work of great breadth by Giovanni Zacchi from Volterra.

On the fourth altar, we find *St. Andrew Le to his Martyrdom* by Francesco Albani, with strong participation of his school (1641); on th fifth one, *Our Lady of Assumption* of the alway lively painter Pietro Faccini (1562-1602) is place above a precious *Virgin with Child*, in Byzantir style donated in 1285 to the Bologna's commu nity by the founder of the Order, St. Filipp Benizi. Finally, on the sixth one, a magnificen classical frame, carved by Formigine, encloses pellucid and radiant *Annunciation* by the follow er of Raphael, Innocenzo da Imola.

The gigantic organ is of modern make and is quite extraordinary for the number of its pip and the variety of its stops.

The *high altar*, a quite complex and overtly
aborated composition, is a Mannerist-styled
ork made by Giovanni Agnolo from Montor-
li, a follower and helper of Michaelangel, from
558 and 1561.

By entering the ambulatory we can find: to the
ft, a melancholy canvas by Alessandro Tiari-
i, representing the *Virgin's Education*
630-1640) and, to the right, the *Tomb at the
oor level of Brother Andrea Manfredi from
aenza*, the Order's General and architect of the
hurch as well, who died in 1396.

We can admire, in the first of the three big
hapels at the back, the most important master-
iece held in the church, the marvellous *En-
roned Virgin with Child and Angels*, (Majesty)
y Cimabue. The soft colouring of the faces has
uggested to critics that the young Duccio di
oninsegna could have also participated in this
ork, and therefore it was dated between 1280
d 1285 when Duccio attended the school of
imabue. The panel was donated by the Pepoli
mily in 1345. Just after the three large chapels,
the apse we can see the relief work represent-

Basilica of S. Maria dei Servi: the façade with the 18th-
ntury square-shaped arcade in the front. 2. The 14th-century
cade flanks the north side of the church. 3. View of the
cade: a portion made by Antonio di Vincenzo. 4. S. Maria
i Servi: its harmonious inside. 5. Cimabue: Madonna with
hild in Majesty (13th century).   5

1

ing *The Virgin with Child between the Saints Lorenzo and Eustachio*, a lovely work by Vincenzo Onofri (1503), a large *terracotta polyptych* of high artistic interest with frescoes by Lippo Dalmasio (end of the 14th century), and the sacristy, which is also quite nice, although its three large canvasses on the altar by Mastelletta (1575-1665) are unfortunately quite blackened.

By walking through the right aisle of the church, we can see: on the sixth altar, the gigantic *Heaven*, a work by Denjs Calvaert of great effect although much too intricate (1602); on the last one, *The Virgin Giving the Habit to the Seven Founders of the Serviti*, an elegant and peaceful work by Marcantonio Franceschini (1648-1729).

Before leaving the church you should pay a brief visit to the external part of the apse terminated in 1437 and to the bell-tower completed in 1453 but modified in 1725. They have also been restored and cleared of later additions in 1927 during renewal works carried out under eng. Guido Zucchini.

Palazzo Carrati, in via Guerrazzi 13, is a building which belonged to the Sanvenanzi in 1525; in 1627 it passed into the hands of the Carrati Counts who had it completely restructured. Vincenzo Maria Carrati (who died in 1675) founded there the **Accademia Filarmonica** (Music Academy) in 1666, which is still active today and quite known throughout the world. Here, on 9th October 1770, Mozart, then fourteen years old, took and passed the admission test for the Academy.

This institution still holds today a large colle tion of mementoes of its past and of famous m sicians. The *corpus* of the whole collection of m sical instruments numbers really exceptior pieces: the mahogany *spinet of Rossini*, built Vienna in 1850; the *sloping desk of Rossini,* 19th century piece of furniture from Bologna; *organ with 360 pipes* of Traeri (1673); the *pia of Ottorino Respighi* made by Fritzmann & So from Vienna; the *piano of Stefano Golinelli* ma by Erard from Paris; the box-wood *music-sta of Stefano Mancinelli*. The collection of oil p traits is quite valuable: the *St. Anthony fro Padua* (the patron Saint of the Academy) is oil canvas by Elisabetta Sirani. *Please contact Director's office for visits to the Academy (t 222997)*.

The continuity of styles in buildings that ha been raised in different centuries, often very d tant one from the other, is assured by the arcad which are the peculiar characteristics of the wh urban layout: the arcade of **Palazzo Hercola** (n.45) acts as a counterpoint to the row of slend columns forming the Servi's arcade. T senatorial home of the Hercolani family, built Architect Angelo Venturoli, who completed it the end of the 18th century, has a scenic gra staircase decorated with statues by Giacomo Maria and the above vault has a fresco, represer ing the apotheosis of Hercules, painted by Fili po Pedrini; the ceremonial hall is painted w a representation of *Apollo with the Hours*, tw rooms were decorated in Chinese style by Vi cenzo Armani and Davide Zanotti, while t room with country scenes is by Rodolfo Fantu zi; the English garden, open to the public, c be reached through via dei Bersaglieri.

In **Palazzo Angelelli** (n. 51), in its first galler shaped courtyard, we can see a statue Prometheus tormented by an eagle by the scul tor Giovanni Battista Bolognini; the ridir ground, planned by Antonio Ambrosi, and off ing an evocative scenic effect onto the garde was also used as a theatre in 1710.

In **Casa Zoppi** (n. 71) too, one of the olde private theatres of the town was set up at the e of the 16th century; in the courtyard we can s a well, whose Doric columns support an arch trave topped by two dolphins, attributed, as the rest of the building, to Antonio Moran called Terribilia.

The 13th-century **Porta** (Gate) at the end strada Maggiore acts as a sort of backdrop to t whole street. This gate was saved from a cor plete destruction by Alfonso Rubbiani, after t elimination in 1903 of the front designed by Car Francesco Dotti. Rubbiani defended with all h might this important medieval building ar stressed the need to save it.

1. *Vitale da Bologna: Madonna of Delivery (14th centur
2. Strada Maggiore Gate: the 14th century big arch. 3. V
S. Vitale starting near St. Bartholomew's. 4. Ravegna
square and the beginning of via S. Vitale.*

Via San Vitale

It seems that Via San Vitale was once called ia Salaria or Salara, because it lay along the oute of the salt merchants going from Ravenna o Bologna. This street still evocates today that emote feeling of fascination, perhaps for the old workshops and stores which dot it and are still faithful to the traditional display of ancient frames, furniture, rare prints and objects.

Palazzo Orsi (ns. 28 and 30) was built in the second half of the 16th century in order to har-

4

1

Palazzo Fantuzzi (n. 23) is certainly the most spectacular one in the street. In 1517 the Fantuzzi family obtained from the «Assunteria d'Ornato», the commission charged with approving or rejecting building projects, the permission to eliminate the arcade from the façade of their house by pledging, as an exchange, to provide it with a beautiful front so as to further improve the town's outlook. The plastic layout of the front is stressed by the device of the strong ashlars covering the half-columns, which outspace the rows of windows, marked by the jutting fastigia; the light and shade interlacing is quite powerful especially in the sudden passages from light to shade in the stones. It is certainly the work of a well-versed artist who knew the avant-garde style of Giulio Romano and Serlio and whom the critics have traditionally identified as Andrea da Formigine. The construction works, which continued up to the end of the 16th century, were carried out by Antonio Tassi, also called Triachini, and afterwards by his son Bartolomeo. In the next century, the Fantuzzi family saw their political power grow quite rapidly and therefore it was necessary to build a scenic *Baroque grand staircase*, commissioned to Paolo Canali (1680); in the trompe-l'oeil perspective there is the *Allegory of the Sun Cart* by Gioachino Pizzoli; the statues of *Hercules, Atlas, Fame, Plenty* and *Prosperity* are by Gabriello Brunelli.

Casa Franchini (n. 31), from the mid-16th century, is linked to the structure of the **Torresotto** (12th-13th centuries), a gate that was part of the second row of the town's walls, also called of the «year one thousand».

monize, at least in the front, two previously erected buildings, which, however, still kept inside their own typical and characteristic layout. This palace has been attributed to Antonio Morandi and it enables us to follow the various stages in the development of the artist who reached his maturity in the magnificent architectonic structure of the Archiginnasio in 1562. Unfortunately, the local sandstone falls easily prey of corrosion which has ruined the elegant friezes of the windows, by blurring the edges of the cartouches and the mermaids' bodies. In the inside, as a background to the garden, a niche holds protectively the precious terracotta work by Domenico Piò (1775), the heroe Hercules choking the Nemean lion. By applying his typical inventive genius, Piò also created a more devout image of the Virgin with Child, a sculpture decorating the 18th-century grand staircase, to be attributed to the school or the followers of the Bibiena family.

Casa Negri (n. 15), an example of Renaissance architecture expressed in a moderate taste, still retains on the entrance door two interesting 16th-century knockers shaped as apotropaic mascarons acting as symbolic guardians of the house. Giovanni Francesco Negri, architect and poet, who translated the Gerusalemme Liberata (The Liberation of Jerusalem) in the dialect of Bologna, founded in this palace the Academy of the Fearless, one of the many private clubs which aimed at giving new impetus to the town's cultural life.

1. Via S. Vitale: Fantuzzi Palace (16th century). 2. Torresotto of S. Vitale (13th century). 3. Church of the Saints Vitale and Agricola in Arena: the 1862 façade. 4. Arcade of the Saints Vitale and Agricola: detail of the portal by Formigine of S. Maria degli Angeli. 5. Roso da Parma: Liuzzi tomb (14th century).

3

CHIESA DEI SANTI VITALE AND AGRICOLA

It seems that this church was built in very ancient times on the remains of the Roman arena
in which the saints Vitale and Agricola had
suffered their martyrdom. However, the first
reliable document attesting its presence as the
parish for the Ravegnana gate quarter dates back
to 1088.

Around the end of the 16th century the church
was completely redone according to the wish of
the Black Benedictine Sisters who ruled over it.
As a consequence, the church's orientation,
which was once from east to west, running
parallel to via S. Vitale, was changed into the
south to north direction, still kept today. The new
place of worship was consecrated in 1641 and underwent extensive restoration works in 1680 (the
main chapel) and, after the Napoleonic period
during which it was suppressed, again in 1824 and
1862 (the inside decoration and the new façade).

The steeple was restructured according to the
design of the architect Agostino Barelli in 1670.

Under the arcade we can see the gravestone
made by Roso da Parma in 1318 for Lucio de'
Liuzzi and for his nephew Mondino, a well famous physician of the Studium of Bologna, considered the father of modern anatomy.

The lovely door of the St. Mary of the Angels'

4

5

129

chapel (decorations by the school of Formigine) is nearby. The square-planned chapel was built around 1497 by Gaspare Nadi and inside we can see: frescoes (*Nativity Scene* and *Angels* around the niche) by Giacomo Francia and (*The Visitation*) by Bartolomeo Ramenghi from Bagnacavallo; a fine canvas (*Flight into Egypt*) by Alessandro Tiarini (1577-1668) and an amazing *Holy Family* modelled in wax and cloth by Angelo Piò (1690-1769).

The altar-piece on the high-altar is quite remarkable: the *Martyrdom of the Saints Vitale and Agricola* was painted in 1872 by Luigi Busi inside the massive carved and gilded wood frame made in 1580 by Giacomo Gentili from a design by the Sicilian architect and painter Tommaso Laureti. The *crypt* is a very evocative place, perhaps because it is the only precious remain of the 11th-century church, brought to light in 1891-92 after a century of neglect during which it had been transformed in a grotto for the adjacent garden of the engineer Giovanni Battista Martinetti.

Palazzo Martinetti (n. 56) was the home of the beautiful Cornelia Rossi, the wife of the architect Martinetti and fancied by Ugo Foscolo, Canova and Byron, who attended her fashionable salon.

Casa Grassi (n. 60), **Casa Grimani** (n. 49) and **Casa Prati** (n. 53) date all back to the 16th century. The last one shows the hand of a very important artist, perhaps Antonio Morandi, also called Terribilia.

Chiesa di S. Maria della Pietà (via S. Vitale 112). The building of this church was started in 1601 under the sponsorship of the Senate of Bologna and various Arts' Guilds. In 1603 the main chapel was consecrated and in 1667 the vaults, designed by the architect Bartolomeo Belli, were built.

The single nave interior characterized by shallow side chapels follows the 16th-century layout typical of Bologna and it is quite austere.

The canvasses with the *Town's Patron Saints* hung on high, date back to the 17th century and come from the St. Lucia's church.

The paintings in the church are quite valuable: in the first two altars on the left, the *Crucifix* and the devout *St. Ann* are works by Bartolomeo Cesi (1556-1629); the *Multiplication of the Loaves and Fishes* is by Lavinia Fontana (1552-1602), while the enamelled work *The Flight into Egypt* in the very ornate fourth chapel is by Andrea Donducci, also called «Mastelletta» (1575-1663) and the *St. Egidio* in the fifth one is by the touching painter Tiarini (1577-1668).

The *Pietà with the Patron Saints of Bologna* in the main chapel, is a copy of the famous painting by Guido Reni, now in the Pinacoteca (Municipal Art Gallery), made by Clemente Albéri in the last century.

By going back along the right side of the church we find again the first altar with the *Annunciation* by Giovanni Luigi Valesio (1579-1640); on the second one the two surreal paintings about the *Miracles of St. Alò* are by Giacomo Cavedoni (1577-1660) and on the last altar we can see the altar-piece representing *St. Ursula with her companions* painted by Bartolomeo Passarotti (1530-1592) along the lines of the more famous *St. Cecilia* of Raphael.

Casa Brogli (n. 55) has a grand staircase planned by Alfonso Torreggiani. If we glance at the side-street on the right, that is Via Begatto, it is possible to see a picturesque section of the old town, characterized by 14th- and 15th century buildings.

Unfortunately, the original Medieval character of *Porta San Vitale* is irretrievably lost considering that its drawbridges were taken away in the 18th century and the defensive avant-corps razed in 1952.

1

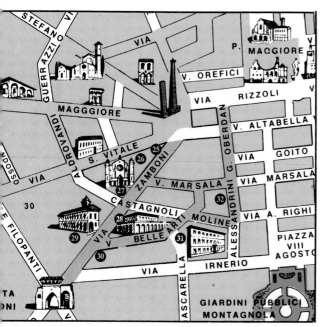

Via Zamboni

Today's via Zamboni was once called San onato street, until it was dedicated (in 1867) to young Jacobin who had tried to stir up a revolt ainst the Pope's rule in 1794. It was a «stra-...», that is a paved street, already an important ...e in the Renaissance period because the palaces the Bentivoglio family, the town's rulers, were cated there together with the rich homes of ...her important families.
Palazzo Malvasia (ns. 14-16), an ancient 13th-...ntury building, was changed in 1760 by Fran-...sco Tadolini according to the architectural con-...pts of Palladio, as we can see in the façade ...pped by a tympanum and spaced by pilaster-

strips. The large arch beside the palace, leading towards via del Carro, has a sandstone masca-ron out of which wine sprung on the people dur-ing festivities and celebration. This was one of the entrances to the Jewish Ghetto;

Palazzo Bianchetti (n. 9) still sports an elegant 16th-century arcade with sandstone capitals shaped as eagles, rams and flowery and greenery decorations. One of the members of this family, Zanna, was one of the lady-in-waiting of the wife of emperor Charles IV (1316-1378). She was also a well-known polyglot.

Palazzo Malvezzi de Medici (n. 13), today's the seat of the Provincial Administration, was known

3

131

once as the «palace of the dark arcade». It was designed by Bartolomeo Triachini in 1560 who rigidly followed and applied the contemporary architectural precepts by overimposing the three Doric, Ionian and Corinthian orders. The imposingly grand staircase is by Francesco Bibiena; the decoration of the «piano nobile» is due to scene and decorative painters from the mid-19th century: Francesco Cocchi, Prospero Pesci, Luigi Samoggia and others. The building looks also onto piazza Rossini, by facing the façade of the church of St. James.

CONSERVATORIO DI MUSICA

In the former Augustinian convent of S. Giacomo Maggiore, dating back to 1267, but redone during the Baroque period (the grand staircase, leading up from the cloister to the upper floor, was built by Alfonso Torreggiani in 1752), the music conservatory «Giovanni Battista Martini» has had its seat since 1804, year in which it became a musical academy. Giovanni Battista Martini, «father Martini», a Franciscan brother from Bologna (1706-1784) was a very learned musician and music expert, a famous book-lover, a composer of lay and sacred music, the author of important texts on the 18th-century music, and chapel-master in St. Francis's. Two collections closely linked to the conservatory were put together or initially started by him. The first one is the **Quadreria di Padre Martini** (paintings' gallery) which had already 80 portraits in 1773 and in 1784 about 300 (others were bought in the 19th and 20th centuries). It is an extraordinary collection of musicians' portraits, famous as well as forgotten ones's, which Martini had put together by having them sent by the musicians themselves for «free». They are placed for the most part in the Sala Bossi, in the rooms of the

music's museum, in the offices and classroom of the conservatory. Several of them are signe by famous painters: *Charles Burney* by S Joshua Reynolds; *Johann Sebastian Bach* t Thomas Gainsborough; *Carlo Broschi, als called Farinello* by Corrado Giaquinto; *Franc sco Maria Zanotti* by William Keeble; *Giusep Corsini*, 1769, and *Ferdinando Gini*, 1759, t Luigi Crespi; *Giovanni Paolo Colonna* t Giovanni Maria Viani; *Giuseppe Santarelli* t Pompeo Batoni; *Antonio Colonna del Corno* t Giuliano Dinarelli; *Giacomo Antonio Arrighi* t Sante Legnani; and many portraits by Ange Crescimbeni among which: *Padre Martini*, *Th mas Christian Walter* (1778), *Jacopo Stecchin Giulio Panziera* (1772), *Philip J. Hinner*, *Valer Tesei*, *Ferdinando Giuseppe Bertoni*, and *Eug nio di Ligniville*. The portrait of *Ludovico Bo tolotti* is by Antonio Muzzi.

The **Civico Museo Bibliografico Musicale** (t civic bibliographical museum of music), whic houses the gorgeous *music's library* whose doo were painted by Giuseppe M. Crespi in 1710-1 was the first music's library in Bologna (1797 This library, which has been set up with precio

---

1. Malvezzi de' Medici Palace by Triachini (16th century 2. Conservatory of music: the old Augustinian portal. 3. Bo Hall with a view of the painting collection of Father Marti

old cabinets and showcases in the *Sala Vecchia* (old room) restored in 1969-72, includes more han 30,000 items, such as manuscripts, illuminated books, printed matters, opera's librettos. The section on madrigalist and church music from the 16th to the 18th centuries is particularly rich. There are many 16th-century music books, with items by Petrucci and Antico. Among the autographs, let us recall the following: Claudio Monteverdi's, Mozart's (he took an exam in order to be admitted to the Philarmonic Academy on 9th October 1770), Rossini's (the music score for the *Barbiere di Siviglia* and a section of the score from the *Stabat Mater*), Callara's, Carissimi's, and Benedetto Marcello's.

The Gallery and the Museum can be visited from 9.30 a.m. to 1 p.m. on weekdays. We recommend you, however, to call first: Conservatory (offices) and Art Gallery, tel. 221483; Museum, tel. 221117.

CHIESA DI S. GIACOMO MAGGIORE

In 1267, the St. Augustin Brothers (or Augustinian hermits) moved here from the town's outskirts where they had been housed in the small church of St. James of Savena twenty years earlier, and started the building of their big church, also dedicated to St. James, over a vast empty lot located just in front of the parish church of St. Cecilia.

In 1315, the main structures of the church were finished and the apse was enlarged in 1341 by the addition of radiating chapels.

The Bentivoglio family, the actual town's rulers, who had their princely palace built in the place where the Municipal Theatre now stands, in the nearby piazza Verdi, in the second half of the 15th century, enriched the church of very important sections. After they had commissioned the building of the family chapel in 1445, they had an outside elegant arcade built between 1478 and 1481, following peaceful Tuscan lines, and finally, between 1493 and 1498, they had the whole inside restructured, by substituting the former wood trusses with three vaults and the small dome still existing now, in a way quite original for Bologna, and by subsequently adding along the sides two rows of chapels which gave the church a clearly Renaissance appearance.

The façade was raised in 1295 by Egidio da Campignano who worked also on the sculptures and the decorations together with Godefrino di Giacomo (they were both from Milan), but the archway above the entrance was later on completely changed. The steeple, originally from the 14th century, was terminated in 1471-1472 with a fine belfry.

The church's inside is endowed by many valuable works of art, very important in order to fully

so fascinating for its silvery tones and the ps
chological solitude of the figures shown throug
a serenely evangelical simplicity, is the maste
piece of Bartolomeo Cesi (1598). The superb Be
tivoglio chapel, a lofty example of a noble fam
ly's chapel in which the 15th-century art in Bolo
gna expresses its best, lies at the end of the aps

This chapel, built in 1445, was enlarged ar
decorated with precious paintings for Giovan
II Bentivoglio between 1488 and 1494. The ma
nificent altar-piece, showing the very elegant i
fluence of Tuscan art, is a masterpiece by Fra
cesco Raibolini, also called «Francia»; the fre
coes, the *Triumphs of Fame and Death* (on t
left) and *Giovanni II with his Wife Ginevra Sfo
za and their Children Before the Virgin wi
Child* (on the right) are all by Lorenzo Costa. I
front of the chapel, the massively-built tomb
Anton Galeazzo Bentivoglio is the precious wo
of Jacopo della Quercia (1371-1438). The ne

grasp the 16th-century painting of Bologna.

On the ninth altar, the crowded *Presentation
to the Temple* is by Orazio Samacchini (1575)
while the other decorations of the chapels are attributed to Agostino Carracci (1557-1602); on the
tenth altar, the *Virgin with Child, St. Nicholas
and Three Young Girls* is by Ercole Procaccini
(1582); and on the eleventh one, the nervous composition by Tiburzio Passarotti (1577), the *Martyrdom of St. Catherine*.

After entering the apse's perimeter, the *Virgin
with Child in Glory with the Saints Benedict,
John the Baptist and Francis* on the first altar,

Manzoli chapel is a work by Giuseppe Mazza (1681) and was the first in Bologna to be complete-ly decorated with relief-works without paintings.

In the following chapels of the apse, we can find, all lined up one after the other: a precious *Crucifix* by Simone dei Crocifissi (1370); an in-valuable *Polyptych* by Paolo Veneziano (ca. 1340); a few fragments of *frescoes* by Cristoforo da Bologna (1360-1375); and another *Polyptych* by Jacopo di Paolo (ca. 1416).

After the sacristy's door, we find the Poggi chapel with refined Mannerist lines made by Pellegrino Tibaldi (1527-1597) who worked in the lateral frescoes as well as in the architecture; *The Baptism of Jesus* over the altar and the decora-tions on the vault are by Prospero Fontana.

In the next second chapel, all the paintings are by Lorenzo Sabatini (1575). Only the *Archangel Michael* in the altar-piece is by Denjs Calvaert.

The third chapel is dominated by the sorrow-ful dialogue with the Heavens of the famous *St. Rocco* by Ludovico Carracci (1602); the contem-porary wall decorations are by Francesco Brizzi.

By continuing along that same side of the church, we can see the following remarkable works: on the fifth chapel, the *Mystical Marri-ge of St. Catherine and Saints* by Innocenzo da Imola (1536) who painted also the graceful *Na-tivity Scene* on the predella; on the seventh one, the pellucid *Enthroned Virgin and Saints with the*

4

135

Clients is a work by Bartolomeo Passarotti (1565) who placed his signature by painting a sparrow on the lower section; *Christ Appearing to St. John from St. Facundo*, majestic work by Giacomo Cavedoni (ca. 1620); the livid *Fall of St. Paul* by Ercole Procaccini (1573) and, finally, in the last chapel near the door the bright *Adoration by the Kings*, a fresco which had been recently found under a Baroque altar-piece, attributable to the minor masters active in the near

1

3

6

by church of St. Cecilia.

The left side of the church is accompanied by a magnificent arcade built in 1477-1481 for Giovanni II Bentivoglio: the building reveals an archeological affinity to the late-Roman art, as can be seen in the pulvins topping the capitals supporting the spans, which can also be found in the arcade of the **Palazzo Pannolini** (n. 18), in whose courtyard there is a statue representing Pallas by Petronio Tadolini. **Palazzo Magnani** (n. 20), today's the seat of the Credito Romagnolo Bank, was built between 1577 and 1590 by Domenico Tibaldi. In its hall there is a 25 metre-long frieze whose partitions are dedicated to the *History of the Foundation of Rome* by the Carracci painters. Each episode, conceived as an individual canvas on an easel, is interspaced by polychromatic figures, the so-called «termini»: the plastic study of the human figure in motion and the attention placed also on the details in the landscape were studied not only by local painters but also foreign ones, therefore attracting young European artists to the Carracci's school in order to learn a particular concept of natural beauty filtered through a Classical ideal.

Chiesa di S. Cecilia. The exact date of the construction of this church is unknown. It was built next to the second row of walls, which can still be seen, at least a section of it, behind the apse.

7

Francesco Raibolini, known as Francia: Madonna with Child and Saints. 2. Lorenzo Costa: The triumph of Fame. Jacopo della Quercia: ark of Anton Galeazzo Bentivoglio. Simone dei Crocifissi: Crucifix from 1370. 5. Jacopo di Paolo: Polyptych of the Crowning of Mary. 6. Pellegrino Tibaldi: The conception of John the Baptist. 7. Under the 15th-century arcade, the 14th-century funerary arks.

We know, however, that in 1323 it went into the hands of the Augustinian brothers, who owned the nearby St. James's church, and who in 1359 commissioned its restoration because it was really dilapidated. Between 1481 and 1483 Gaspare Nadi raised the floor of the small church in order to bring its level up to the one of the new outside arcade, which had just recently been terminated. He also built the big bevelled barrel vault which can still be seen today.

Between 1505 and 1507, Giovanni II Bentivoglio had the church decorated with a series of frescoes narrating the lifes of St. Cecilia and St. Valerianus which represent one of the highest examples of the Renaissance painting in Bologna and which are the passage from the certainties of the 15th-century art to the doubts and anxiety so typical of the 16th century.

The «tales» start at the side of the altar on the left wall: the *Wedding of Valerianus and Cecilia* by Francesco Raibolini, also called «Francia», in which the reference to the art of Raphael is not only a purely formal one; the *Conversion of Valerianus* by Lorenzo Costa, the last work made in Bologna by the painter before moving to Mantova, where he was going to take the office of court painter, previously held by Mantegna; the *Baptism of Valerianus*, in which the Mannerist figures on the foreground are by Giacomo and Giulio Francia while the magnificent background and the affected far-away figures are by Amico Aspertini; *An Angel Crowns the Two Newly-wed* by Amico Aspertini, in which the formal geometrical solutions melt away in a restless melancholy; the *Martyrdom of the Saints Valerianus and Tiburtius* by Amico Aspertini, one of his more typical and known works, in which the

painter, by working through an archeologist outlook precociously assumed during a recent journey to Rome, tried to merge the harmonious styles of Tuscany and Umbria with the «treacherous» ones of Germany; the *Burial of the Saints Valerianus and Tiburtius* by Amico Aspertini; *S. Cecilia in front of the Prefect Almachius* of difficult attribution, perhaps by Giovanni Maria Chiodarolo after a design of Aspertini; *Martyrdom of St. Cecilia* by Cesare Tamaroccio with the hand of Aspertini in the group of figures in the left; the *Alms of St. Cecilia* by Lorenzo Costa, an harmonious composition revealing a quiet and peaceful feeling; the *Burial of St. Cecilia* by Francesco Francia, an exquisite work notable for its internal composition.

Palazzo Malvezzi-Campeggi (n. 22) was built in the mid 16th century for the Malvezzi, the fiercely rival family of the Bentivoglio, who had been exiled from Bologna in 1488 and were readmitted back only after the troops of Pope Julius II had defeated Giovanni II. The architecture of this noble home sports a sophisticated decorative device on the stones so as to make them as if they had been cut in rosette shapes. The tradition attributes the building of this palace to Andrea and Giacomo da Formigine: the counterpart of the outside arcade is the elegant inside courtyard with two-tiered overlying open galleries; the statue

---

1. Church of S. Cecilia: Baptism of Valerian, attributed Giacomo and Giulio Francia. 2. Lorenzo Costa: Conversion of Valerian. 3. Municipal Theatre, inaugurated in 1763.

representing Hercules, is by Giuseppe Mazza. In the inside rooms, tempera paintings by Carlo Lodi and Antonio Rossi can still be seen.

The **Teatro Comunale** (Municipal Theatre at n. 30), built by Antonio Bibiena over the place where the *Domus Aurea* of the Bentivoglio family had once stood before being destroyed in 1507, was inaugurated in 1763 with the performance of an opera by Gluck: *Il trionfo di Clelia*. The theatre includes four tiers of boxes and a gallery: the original plan by Bibiena, which was not approved, showed an original avant-garde solution, as is still possible to see in the simple wood model. An extensive and complete renovation in the utility rooms, in the scenes and theatrical equipment was carried out in the first decades of the 19th century by Giuseppe Tubertini while the decoration was completely redone by Luigi Busi and Luigi Samoggia in 1866. Finally, the façade was completed in 1933 by Umberto Rizzi.

Palazzo Salaroli (n. 25) dates back to the Benivoglio's times; It has a porched courtyard, frescoes from the 15th and 16th centuries and a 15th-century staircase.

Chiesa di S. Sigismondo. This church was already mentioned at the end of the 13th century and its name was soon linked to the one of the Malvezzi noble family who lived in the nearby «Ca' granda» (big house), today's used by the University. Gaspare Malvezzi had the church completely restructured in 1450 and the Marquess Sigismondo Malvezzi had it completely rebuilt between 1725 and 1728 according to the design of the architect Carlo Francesco Dotti who tried to mask the extreme narrowness of the place by simplifying the external lines and curving the inside surfaces.

The church's single nave was further reduced by four side altars built by the architect Giuseppe Jarmorini in 1792. The decorations in the vault are quite nice: they were made in 1870 by Napoleone Angiolini, a figure-painter, and by Michele Mastellari, an ornamentalist painter, and represent the *Glorification of St. Luigi Gonzaga* and the *Communion of the Blessed Imelda Lambertini*, whose remains are kept in the richly decorated side ark (by Architect don Angelo Raule, 1940).

The small bell-tower was raised in 1795 according to a design by Architect Angelo Venturoli.

2

PALAZZO POGGI
E MUSEI UNIVERSITARI

Palazzo Poggi, in via Zamboni 3, has been the central seat of the University and the Rector's office since 1803. It was built between 1549 and 1560 following a design by Pellegrino Tibaldi and/or Bartolomeo Triachini as the noble and sumptuous home for Alessandro Poggi and his brother, the Cardinal Giovanni. It is magnificent-y decorated inside (the frescoes portraying mithological and Biblical scenes are by Pellegrino Tibaldi, and the ones with landscapes and scenes from everyday life are by Nicolò dell'Aate). The *Tower of the Specola* rises above it: t was started in 1712-13 according to a plan by Giuseppe Antonio Torri and was completed by Carlo Francesco Dotti in 1723-25. At that time, Palazzo Poggi became the seat of the *Institute of Sciences*, according to the will of Luigi Ferlinando Marsigli, who had founded it in 1711 nd inaugurated in 1714. At the opening of the

. *The Municipal Theatre: Bibiena's Room. 2. Verdi square, etween the Municipal theatre and the old Bentivoglio stales; the Specola tower rises beyond Paleotti Palace. 3. Veri square with the Walls of the year one thousand and the eeples of St. Cecilia's and St. James'. 4. The Specola Tower in an old etching. 5. Palazzo Poggi, the University's headuarter: the magnificent courtyard.*

4

141

1

arcade from Largo Trombetti we can see the symbol of Bologna's old student fraternity, the marble *fittone delle Spaderie*, a kerbstone placed in 1870 in the Spaderie street, no longer existing now. The «fittone» was placed where it now stands in 1912. It was restored in 1984.

The building houses, besides many University's offices and institutes, rooms and exhibits of exceptional interest especially for their scientific and cultural value. The itineraries established for a thorough visit of these important exhibits start at the ground floor, from the *Carducci Lecture Hall*, in which the great Poet had held his classes on Italian literature from 1860 onward, for 43 years. Here we can see the old desks occupied by many famous students, here the flamboyant author of the «Odi Barbare» is portrayed in a bronze bust made in Rome by Bastianelli. The room facing this lecture hall is called the *Hercules Room* because the restored sandstone statue of Hercules, sculpted by Angelo Piò around 1730 and placed up to a few years back in the courtyard to which it gave its name, was later on placed here (a copy was put on the old pedestal). The tour of the museums of Palazzo Poggi offers the visitor the invaluable scientific and cultural contribution given by the Institutes of Sciences of Bologna (which had been active in this location for the whole 18th century) through its laboratories and historical collections out of which the majority of the Bologna University's museum, including the scientific ones, have sprung up. They form one of the most important institutions of this kind in Italy and abroad.

The **Museo storico dello studio** (the Historical Museum of the Studium), established for the University's eight hundredth anniversary in 1888, includes more than 250 documents, many mementoes (let us recall the Rector's insignia from the 16th century and Luigi Galvani's robe), and several portraits. The **Museo delle Navi** (Ships' Museum) and the **Collezione delle antiche carte geografiche** (Museum of Ancient Maps) are closely linked to the establishment of the *Ge-*

5

6

...raphical and Nautical Room* (1724): the first
...e presents ten very rare models of warships
...m the 17th and 18th centuries, such as *Le Roy-
...Louis, Le Bien Aimé* (1771) and *Le Vainqueur*;
...e second museum exhibits important maps, en-
...aved on copper, from the 17th century pub-
...hed in Bologna, Paris, Marseille, Amsterdam
...d in England.
Next to the Ships' Museum we can find the
...mera di Architettura Militare (Military Ar-
...itecture Room, divided up into two rooms)
...ked to the military career of Marsigli and to
...s unquenching thirst for knowledge. The first

...*Giosuè Carducci's lecture hall. 2. Rectoral insignia from*
...*Studium, 16th century. 3. Boats' Museum: Le Bien Aimé.*
...*The Royal Louis, a 1630 model. 5. Le Vainqueur. 6 and*
...*Room of military architecture: models of fortified towns*
...*tail).*

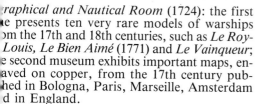

7

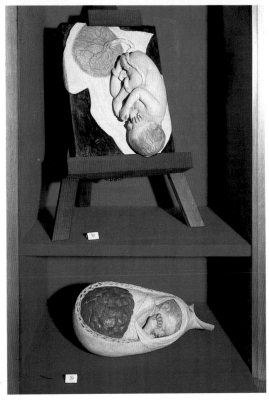

room is dominated at its centre by a big mod of the town of Breisach; there are also oth models of strongholds, a *vernetta*, a *milita bridge*, an *ammunition cart*, large water-coloure panels and various models of old guns and mo tars.

The **Museo Ostetrico «Giovanni Antonio Ga li»** (Obstetrics Museum) is housed in the ne rooms. It was founded in 1757 for Pope Benedi XIV, who had bought the scientific equipmer of the famous surgeon Galli (1708-1782). Th Museum is the reconstruction of an experimer tal laboratory, very exceptional for those time which attests of the very high levels reached b obstetrics in the 18th century. There are also ana tomical tables, clay, wood and wax models, an surgical instruments.

The **Museo di etnografia indiana e orienta** (Museum of Eastern and Indian Ethnograph has been recently rearranged. It was previous located in a section of the Archiginnasio raze during W. W II. It is formed by the items d nated to the town by the scientist and patriot, S nator Francesco Pullé (1850-1934) which are ve valuable for their artistical and historical impo

---

1 and 2. A room of the Obstetrics Museum and two mod by Giovanni Antonio Galli. 3 and 4. Astronomy Museu old instruments (armillary sphere and telescope). 5. The mer ian room in the Specola Tower (detail).

4

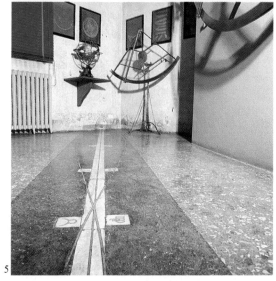

5

tance. In the Rector's offices and in the University's Library, there is an important **paintings' Exhibition** with more than 600 valuable portraits, a collection started in 1754 with the 403 pieces bequeathed by Cardinal Filippo Maria Monti from Bologna. It includes portraits of cardinals, theologians, scientists, philologists, jurists, and men of letters; the authors are for the most part unknown. Let us mention the following: *Francesco Zanotti* by William Keeble; *Ludovico M. Montefani*, attributed to Angelo Crescimbeni; *Marco Antonio Collina Sbaraglia* by Donato Creti; *Self-portrait* by Lucia Casalini Torelli; *Giovanni Antonio Galli* by Crescimbeni; *Luigi Ferdinando Marsigli* by an unknown author, all of them in the Library. Also: *Benedict XIV* attributed to Carlo Vandi; *Eustachio Zanotti* attributed to Giampiero Zanotti; *Eustachio Manfredi*, a marble bust by Ercole Lelli; *Self-portrait* also by Ercole Lelli; *Laura Bassi* by Carlo Vandi; *Self-portrait* also by Vandi, all of them in the Rector's offices and in the Museums.

The **Museo di Astronomia** (Museum of Astronomy) is in the small tower and in the meridian room of the **Specola** (the entrance is at n. 31); it documents the progress in the observation of celestial bodies through a series of precious instruments used in the 18th and 19th centuries by the astronomers of the Institute of Sciences. Some of them had belonged to Marsigli. In the meridian room, set up in 1726, the following items are of remarkable interest: the brass and marble *meridian line* by Ercole Lelli (1741), the *nobile quadrant* by Lusverg (1703), the *mobile quadrant* by Menini (1710), a *string meridian*

from 1726, a *clock* by Quare (17th century), a *wall quadrant* by Sisson (1739). In the small tower, the evolution of the astronomic observation is attested by various instruments, such as the brass 16th-century *surveyor's cross*, a *plane astrolabe* (1565) by Gualtiero of Louvain, a *theodolite* by Paul Carré (17th century), a *sun-dial* by Bion from France (18th century), the eight metre *telescope* by Campani (17th century), and the *passages' instrument* (1739) by Jonathan Sisson from London. In the 18th century the imposing *Assembly Hall* of the Institute of Sciences was built right next to the northern flank of

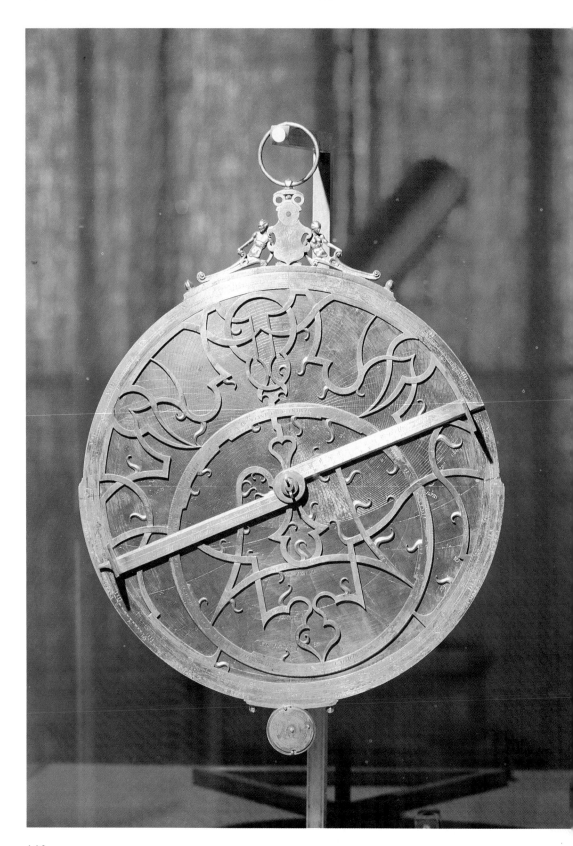

...alazzo Poggi. Planned by Dotti, it was inaugu-...ted in 1756 after two decades of works. It is ...section of the **Biblioteca Universitaria** (Univer-...y's library) with entrance at n. 35, which com-...ises now more than 900,000 volumes and in-...luable series of codices, manuscripts, incuna-...la, prints and drawings. The library includes ...so two precious scientific museums. The first ...ne is the **Museo Aldrovandi**, set up here in 1907, ...hich exhibits in 18th-century show-cases rare ...dy materials collected by the famous naturalist ...isse Aldrovandi from Bologna (1522-1605) and ...presents the remains of that first «museum» ...6th century) already open to the public in the ...th century in Palazzo Pubblico. The water-...loured panels are gorgeous, and the cut wood ...ocks for printing are also quite interesting. ...mong the scientific items, let us recall the fa-...ous *Ranina Aldrovandi* (Aldrovandi's frog). ...ne **Museo Marsigli**, set up in 1930, is connect-... with the Aldrovandi's one: it exhibits docu-...ents of the scientific activity of the great scien-...t from Bologna.

The University's museums in Palazzo Poggi ...hone 259021-259022-259023-259030) are open ...ery day (Monday excluded) from 9.30 a.m. to

...A 16th-century astrolabe made by Gualtiero, the nephew ... Gemma Frisio. 2. Carlo Francesco Dotti: main assembly ...l of the Science Institute. 3. Marsigli Museum, with the ...onument dedicated to the scientist.

3

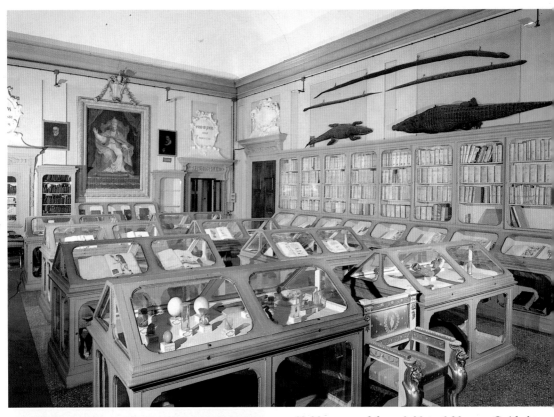

12.30 p.m. and from 3.30 to 6.30 p.m. Guided tour on booking (tel. n. 512151).

Museo di geologia e paleontologia «Giovanni Capellini» (Museum of Geology and Paleontology), in via Zamboni 63, is located in the rooms of the old Azzolini Hospital. Inaugurated in 1881, it is dedicated to the famous geologist and paleontologist from La Spezia (1833-1922), who was also rector of the university. It exhibits many important items from the collections of Aldrovandi (who founded the first museum of natural history in 1556), of Ferdinando Cospi (17th century) and Marsigli. Some show-cases date back to the 18th century. Among the items, all of exceptional quality, we would like to mention the following: fossils and rocks from the *Museum Metallicum* of Aldrovandi, already open to the public in 1648, an *Ichthyosaurus quadriscissus* from Germany; a *Mastodon alvernensis*; an *Ursus spelaeus* from Venezia Giulia; a *Glyptodon Typus* from Argentina; a *celidoterium capellinii* from South America; a giant model of *Diplodocus carnegiei*. Among the items from Bologna: remains of *Cetoteriophanes*, a whale from the Pliocene, from S. Lorenzo in Collina, and the sirenid *Felsinotherium forestii*, from Rio sto di Pianoro. The Museum hosts 150,000 specimens of invertebrates, 200 of vertebrates, 6,000 fossil plants, 15,000 rocks. To visit, phone 35455.

Museo di mineralogia e petrografia «Luigi Bombicci» (Museum of Mineralogy and Petro

2

5

phy), piazza di Porta S.Donato, 1. Located in 1903 building (Engineer Pasquale Penza), it was set up in 1862 by Luigi Bombicci Porta who arranged also the collections. It is basically divided up into three sections: general mineralogy, with over 5,000 items and collections of meteorites and semi-precious stones; Regional collections with over 12,000 specimens; sedimentary, magmatic and metamorphic rocks, and specimens of interest in the field of mining and studies of deposits. The collections of amber and precious stones are also of high quality. *For visits, please call n. 243556.*

Museo di zoologia (Museum of Zoology), via Francesco Selmi, 1; tel. n. 354188. It also comes originally from the collections of Aldrovandi (1556) with the addition of other collections made by Giuseppe and Gaetano Monti, by Camillo Ranzani and others. It still has the original layout arranged by Alessandro Ghigi who placed in this building from 1933 the old collections, the ones from the 19th century and the contemporary ones. The following items are of particular importance: the *fish collection* made by Ranzani, the *coral collection* of Marsigli, the *taxidermist preparaions* from the laboratory (the *moonfish*

Aldrovandi Museum in the Benedict XIV room. 2. A valuable fossil: the «Aldrovandi small frog». 3. Zoology Museum: ibex and chamois in the diorama of Gran Paradiso. 4. black bear, in the Abruzzo Park's diorama. 5. The entrance hall, with the Rhinoceros Unicornis and the Moonfish.

and the *one-horn rhinoceros* are quite remarkable specimens), the italian birds' collection of Zaffagnini-Bertocchi, the *humming birds' collection* of Pius IX, the *shell collection* of Attilio Giovanardi, etc. The diorama and the teaching aids' collections have a high scientific interest. The big «sfargide» or *lute tortoise* is a gift from Benedict XIV. Phone 251723-354188

Museo di antropologia (Museum of Anthropology), via Francesco Selmi, 1. Founded in 1908 by the famous anthropologist Fabio Frassetto, it exhibits a vast number of osteology materials of scientific interest to be used for educational purposes, by giving examples of the fundamental stages of the evolution process and the prehistoric cultures from the lower Paleolithic to the Neolithic: masks, models of busts, models of fossil primates, collections of skeletons of non-extint primates. There are also many specimens from the Region and the area of Bologna in particular. Phone 354209.

Museo di anatomia comparata «Ercole Giacomini» (Museum of Comparative Anatomy), via Belmeloro 8. Set up in 1807 with the preparations of the famous physicians Germano Azzoguidi, Antonio Alessandrini and Gaetano Gandolfi, it exhibits preparations for injection (in coloured wax) of the arterial and venous system of mammals, and it has also a large exhibit of vertebrates' skeletons such as the one of the *Physeter macrocefalus*, a 20 metre-long sperm whale.

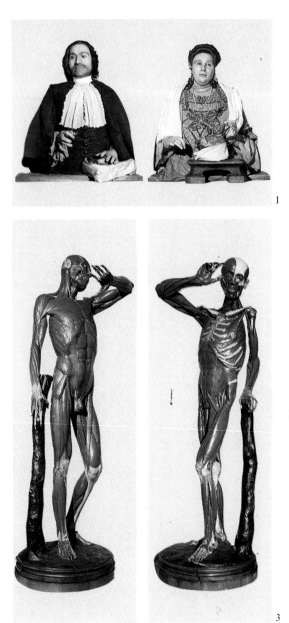

1

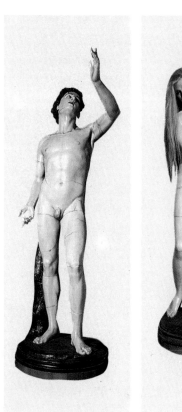

2

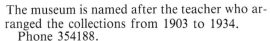

3

The museum is named after the teacher who arranged the collections from 1903 to 1934.

Phone 354188.

Museo di anatomia degli animali domestici (Museum of Domestic Animals), via Belmeloro 12, established on the older *Museum of Veterinary* of Giacomo Gandolfi (1784), it was arranged by Clemente Papi in 1882 and later on improved and developed. It includes about two thousand anatomical preparations relative to all the tracts of domestic animals; many of these date back to the 18th and 19th centuries. The **Museo di patologia generale e anatomia patologica veterinaria** (Museum of Veterinary General

Pathology and Pathologic Anatomy), via Be meloro 10, phone number 243078-243212 (wit beautiful full-size plastic models in wax, clay an plaster) and **Raccolte dell'istituto di patolog speciale e clinica chirurgica veterinaria** (Collec tions of the Institute of Special Pathology an Veterinary Surgery's teaching hospital), via Quirico Filopanti 9, are naturally linked to th above-mentioned museum.

Museo di anatomia umana normale (Museur of Normal Human Anatomy), via Irnerio 48. was firstly formed by the *collection of anatom cal waxworks*, teaching aids that knew phenomenal blooming in Bologna in the 18t century, linked to the fact that it was then almo impossible for anatomy students to study on re bodies. The museum is usually called the *wa museum* because it exhibits the famous creation of wax artists who worked on live models. It wa first set up as the *anatomy theatre of the Inst tute of Sciences* (1742) by Pope Benedict XIV The Pope commissioned various anatomic: pieces to the sculptor and anatomist Ercole Lel (1702-1766), after having seen his two famou panels (shown here) of a *Normal kidney* and *Horseshoe kidney*. The following works are ma; nificent under an artistic point of view: the grou of eight full-size *statues of skinned people*, whic illustrate the bundles of muscles running und€ the skin of men and women, displayed in beau

ful 18th-century show-cases (it seems that for *Adam* and *Eve* Lelli was aided by Domenico Piò and Ottavio Toselli while Giovanni Manzolini participated in the creation of the other wax-works); by Anna Morandi Manzolini: *Self-portrait* (a bust) and the *Bust of her Husband, Giovanni Manzolini*, besides the really famous, and rightly so, *Hands*; by Giovanni Manzolini: the *Foetus with funicle and placenta*. The 19th-century waxworks by Clemente Susini and Giuseppe Astorri are also quite excellent. The museum was placed in here in 1907. The *Calori Collection* is also located in this building: thou-and skulls from different periods and locations, which had been arranged and studied by the famous anatomist Luigi Calori (1807-1896): one of them is thought to be the skull of Athalarich, son of Amalasunta (the skeleton wore a medal of the Gothic king) and was therefore «authenticated» by Cardinal Oppizzoni after it was found in 1838 in Barbianello on the hills around Bologna. Phone 351691.

Museo di fisica (Museum of Physics), via Irerio 46, tel. 351099. It illustrates the history of physical sciences from the 18th century up to

«Wax museum»: busts of the Manzolini family by Anna Morandi Manzolini. 2. Ercole Lelli: Adam and Eve. 3. Ercole Lelli: Outer-laying and inner-laying muscles. 4. Botanical Institute built by Collamarini (1916). 5. Botanical Garden: exotic plants in the greenhouse.

5

now, by stressing the link between the more recent equipment and the old devices in relation to mechanics, optics and acoustics. The following instruments are quite interesting: the *optical laboratory* of Giuseppe Campani (17th century), the *dark room* of Adams (18th century), the *planetarium* of Adams-Ferguson, a *model of a locomotive* from 1857, the 18th-century *teaching and experimental instruments* from the laboratories of Lord George Cowper, Augusto Righi and Quirino Majorana.

Orto botanico and erbario (Botanical Garden and Herbarium), via Irnerio 42, tel. 351301. Established in 1568 by Ulisse Aldrovandi, thus realizing a project by Luca Ghini, this garden was placed inside the Palazzo Pubblico and Terribilia made for it a tank that can be seen today in the Pinacoteca.

In 1803 it was moved to its present location near the Bentivoglio's Palazzina della Viola in accordance to a plan for a new University *campus* elaborated by Giovanni Battista Martinetti. In older times it was called *Garden of the simple* because only medicinal plants, called *simple medicines* (that is produced directly from plants), were grown there. Its present layout was arranged by Nicolò Giosuè Scannagatta and was further improved by the famous botanist Antonio Bertoloni in the 19th century. It includes more than 2,000 species, of which many are grown under environmental conditions reproducing their places of origin. They are all extremely interesting: the Gymnosperm plants, medicinal plants from Italy, the wooded park, plants of the Mediterranean Region, the ornamental garden, fresh water environment, the Appennines' mesic woods, tropical plants and the magnificent green-house with the collection of cacti and succulents. The *Herbarium* includes several thousand specimens of dried plants: it is a collection known throughout Europe and it hosts also specimens dried by Aldrovandi in the 16th century, the large 18th-century collection of Giuseppe Monti, and the

hortus siccus florae italicae - dried garden herb of Italy - (with 30,000 specimens).

Museo di anatomia e istologia patologica «Cesar Taruffi» (Museum of Pathologic Histology an Anatomy), via Massarenti 9, tel. 308991: *it can b visited on Mondays and Wednesdays from 9 a.m to 12.30 p.m. and on Saturdays from 10 a.m. to p.m. (please call first).* Started up on the 18th and 19th centuries, it was placed here in 1948, and later restructured and rearranged by Prof. Pao lo Scarani in 1983. It comprises mostly specimen and research studies on teratology (that is mal formations) by the famous anatomist and pathol ogist Cesare Taruffi (Bologna 1821-1902); it ex hibits many preparations in formalin or in sic co, and nice anatomical waxworks by Giuseppe Astorri and Cesare Bettini.

Palazzo Gorrieri (n. 34) contains a grand stair case by Angelo Venturoli (1791) with sculture by Bonaventura Furlani.

Palazzo Riario (n. 38) sports an arcade and a hall decorated with 16th-century capitals.

In via **Belmeloro**, which according to tradition was named after a beautiful laurel tree (alloro growing there, there is the seat of **Johns Hop kins University from the U.S.A.**, inaugurated in 1962 and located in a building, especiall designed for it by Architect Enzo Zacchiroli.

At the end of via Zamboni we can see **Port San Donato** (San Donato Gate), originally from the 13th century, with a drawbridge added in 1354. After the razing of the town's walls (1903 the gate stood, and still does, alone.

Via Belle Arti

Via Belle Arti, once called Borgo della Paglia (Straw Quarter), derives its name from the Arts' Academy founded in 1878 and located in this street.

PINACOTECA NAZIONALE

The Pinacoteca Nazionale, the most important Picture Gallery in Bologna, is located in via Belle Arti 56, in the former Jesuits' monastery of St. Ignatius. In another section of this vast monastery the Arts' Academy is located which includes also the Baroque church of St. Ignatius. In 1796, the Bologna's Senate unified in a public collection housed in the Arts' Academy all the paintings from the suppressed churches and convents (together with the ones already belonging to the Institute of Sciences) in order to stop their probable transfer to France. Therefore, today's Picture Gallery was born. It was at first housed in the former monastery of Saints Vitale and

Agricola. The new Gallery was moved to the former Jesuit seminary built by Torreggian (1726-27) on 20th September 1803. Greatly im proved by bequests, donations and acquisition (in 1882 it became autonomous from the Acade my), it is today one of the most important galler ies in Europe, and it illustrates with great clarit and accomplishment the development of th painting schools of Bologna throughout the cen turies together with invaluable examples of othe schools and styles from Italy and abroad. Th arrangement slowly unravels this continuou historical thread and, while it places a strong im portance on the highest quality pieces, neverthe less it shows the average cultural level and civili zation quality typical of Bologna and reached here from the 14th to the 18th centuries. In th

---

1. National Picture Gallery. Vitale da Bologna: St. George and the dragon.

courtyard we can see the famous *tank* by Francesco Terribilia, taken from the Garden of Simple in the Palazzo Comunale (Municipal Palace - see photo at pag. 30). The staircase hall, whose vault was painted with a line of arcades in perspective (18th century), displays a large canvas by Gaetano Gandolfi, *The Marriage in Cana* (1775).

Section of Primitive Artists. Room I (Primitive artists from Bologna): a big *Crucifix* by a follower of Giunta Pisano, also called «Master of the Crucifix of S. Maria del Borgo» from the 13th century; *St.George and the Dragon*, a marvellous panel by Vitale da Bologna, ca. 1335-40; also by Vitale, four *Tales of St. Anthony Abbot*, and the *Crowning of the Virgin*; also: the *Prayer in the Garden of Getsemane* by Cristoforo da Bologna; *Tales of the Virgin and Four Saints*, a small altar-piece by Cristoforo da Bologna; a *Crucifixion* and other works by Simone dei Crocifissi. Room II: *Crowning of the Virgin* by Lippo Dalmasio; three small panels with *Figures of Saints* by Jacopo di Paolo; big *Crucifixion* by Giovanni da Modena.

Giotto's Room: a *Virgin with Child and Angels* by Lorenzo Monaco; a large Polyptych with the *Enthroned Virgin and Saints* signed by Giotto and partly painted by his school, dated between 1333-34; small panels with *St. Anthony Abbot* and *St. Bartholomew* by Lorenzo Veneziano.

Room of Crucifixes, with 15th-century paintings linked to the 14th-century Gothic tradition. In particular let us mention two large *Crucifixes* by Michele di Matteo, a polyptych by Pietro Lianori, 1443, with the *Enthroned Virgin and Saints*. **14th- and 15th Century Frescoes Hall**. *The Last Supper and Four Saints* by Vitale da Bologna, 1340; a fragment of a *Resurrection* by Vitale; a gorgeous *St. James at the Battle of Clavijo* from the first half of the 14th century by a Master called the Pseudo-Jacopino

Room of the Frescoes from Mezzaratta brought here from their original location. The big fresco at the back of the room is by Vitale (*Annunciation, Nativity Scene, Miracle, Dream of the Virgin*); on the right wall there are frescoes by Jacopo di Paolo and Simone dei Crocefissi (*Tales of the Life of Christ*); on the left wall frescoes by Jacopo da Bologna and Jacopo Avanzi (*Tales of St. Joseph and Moses*).

Renaissance Section: a *Polyptych*, 1450, by Antonio and Bartolomeo Vivarini; *St. Jerome* by Marco Zoppo; *Altar-piece of the Merchants*, an extraordinary piece by Francesco del Cossa from 1472; a *Virgin with Child and Two Saints* by Lorenzo Costa from 1496; an exceptional *Crying Mary*, a fragment of a fresco by Ercole Roberti. A collection of works by Francia, such as the *Scappi Madonna*, the *Felicini Altar-piece* (1494), the *Madonna of the Manzoli*, a *Dead Christ Held by Two Angels*. A *Wedding of the Virgin* by Lorenzo Costa; the *Apprenticeship* altar-piece by Amico Aspertini. The *Ecstasy of St. Cecilia with the Saints Paul, John the Evangelist, Augustin and Mary Magdalene* by Raphael is a really well-known masterpiece. It was commissioned in 1515 by the blessed Elena Duglioli Dall'Olio for the church of S. Giovanni in Monte. A *Virgin with Child and Saints* by Perugino, ca. 1495; *Adoration of the Child* by Garofalo. 16th-century works from Emilia and Romagna: the famously refined *Madonna of St. Margaret* by Parmigianino. Among the artists from foreign schools: *The Last Supper* by El Greco, ca. 1567; *The Virgin of the Rose Bush* by Martin Schongauer; a small altar with *Esther and Ahassuerus* and on the doors *Adam* and *Eve* of the Pseudo-Civetta.

Mannerist Room: *Supper of St. Gregorius Magnus* by Vasari; *Deposition* by Prospero Fontana; *Crowning of the Virgin and Saints* by Guido Reni; *Resurrection of Christ* and *Presentation to the Temple* by Bartolomeo Passarotti.

Carracci Room: by Agostino, *Communion of St. Jerome* and the *Virgin's Assumption*; by Annibale, the *Annunciation* in two panels, *Madonna*

1. National Picture Gallery: The Crucifix of S. Maria del Borgo (13th century; see at page 152). 2. Vitale da Bologna: small panel with two stories of St. Anthony Abbot. 3. Giotto and his workshop: Polyptych. 4. Marco Zoppo: St. Jerome the penitent.

a of Ludovico, *Assumption of the Virgin*; by
Ludovico, *Conversion of St. Paul*, *Scalzi Madonna*, *Bargellini Madonna*, the famous *Sermon of John the Baptist*, and the *Martyrdom of St. Ursula*.

Baroque and 18th-Century Section. Guido Reni's Room: *Model of the Four Rivers' Fountain* by Bernini, 1650; famous canvasses by Guido Reni: the *Beggars Altar-piece*, the nice *Victorious Samson*, *St. Sebastian*, the exceptional *Slaughter of the Innocent* (about 1611), the *Crucifixion with Mary Magdalene and Grieving People*, *St. Andrea Corsini*, the *Pallione of the Plague*. In the following rooms, these works are also very interesting: the *Martyrdom of St. Angel* and the *Tacconi family* by Ludovico Carrac-

3

4

ci; the *Toilet of Venus* and the *Mocked Christ* by Annibale Carracci; *Saints Irene and Sebastian* by Guercino; *Portrait of the Mother* and *Portrait of an Old Lady* by Guido Reni; *Portrait of Young Girls with a Cat and a Rose Branch* by Giuseppe M. Crespi; a magnificent *Deposition* and a dramatic *Burial of the Virgin* by Alessandro Tiarini; *St. William of Aquitaine* by Guercino (1620); *St. Peter Martyr* by Guercino; *Portrait of Cardinal Ferdinando I Gonzaga* and *St. Peter Martyr* by Domenichino; *Susannah and the Old Men* by Simone Cantarini; several canvasses by the powerful painter Mastelletta, such as the *Alms of a Saint Soman*, ca. 1610, and *Christ attended to by Angels*, ca. 1615; an important work by Titian in his old age, the *Crucified Christ and the Good Thief*, probably dating back to ca. 1565.

Crespi Room: the following precious paintings

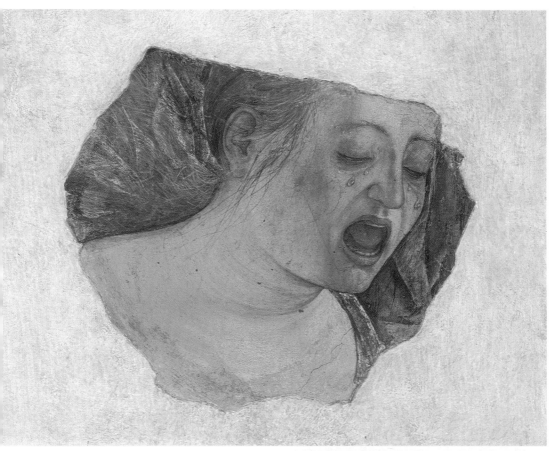

re by Giuseppe M. Crespi: *St. John the Nepomucene, Self-portrait*, the *Mocked Christ, Virgin with Child in Glory, Latona Changes the Shepherds into Frogs*, the famous *Homestead*, the *Slaughter of the Innocent*, the famous *Hunter*, the *Zanobi-Troni family*, the *Slumber of the Cupids*, and *St. Ursula*. The well-known *Portrait of the Canon Luigi Crespi* is by Antonio Crespi. By Luigi Crespi is the *Portrait of a Young Architect*.

Room of the Altar-Pieces or *Teaching room*: *Baptism of Christ* by Francesco Albani; *Virgin of the Rosary* and *Martyrdom of St. Ursula* by Domenichino; the *Carthusian St. Bruno* by Guercino; *Virgin with Child and Saints* by Carlo Cignani; *Transfiguration* by Ludovico Carracci; *Grieving over the Body of Christ*, an unfinished canvas by Federico Barocci.

Room of Niccolò dell'Abate: eight frescoes transferred on canvas are to be seen hanging here. These *Tales from the epic poem Orlando Furio-*

1. The room with the Mezzaratta frescoes. 2. Francesco del Cossa: Merchants'altarpiece. 3. Ercole Roberti: fragment of his Crying Magdalene. 4. Francia: the dead Christ held by two angels.

4

157

were painted by Niccolò around 1550 for the orfanini Palace.

The **Gabinetto dei Disegni e delle Stampe** (the rawings' and Prints' Cabinet) is also part of the icture Gallery. It comprises a collection of over ,000 items, including 81 volumes of etchings nated by Benedict XIV.

The National Picture Gallery is open from 9 m. to 2 p.m. during the week; on holidays from a.m. to 1 p.m.; it is closed on Mondays and holidays falling during the week. To visit the rints' Study, please contact the Gallery's Adinistration.

Palazzo Bianconcini (n. 42), whose 15thntury structure was renewed by Francesco idolini (1770), is still decorated on the grand aircase with frescoes by Pietro Scandellari and the rooms with mythological representations *Bacchus and Ariadne* painted by Gian ioseffo Dal Sole and Enrico Haffner. In the her rooms there are paintings by Gaetano Ganilfi and Pietro Fancelli and decorations by useppe Mazza.

Via Centotrecento (second street on the right via Belle Arti). The toponomy of this street still quite uncertain, perhaps it comes from the angling of an older name derived, as some peo-

Raphael Sanzio: Exstasy of St. Cecilia. 2. Domenico Theoopulos, called El Greco: The Last Supper. 3. Ludovico rracci: Bargellini Madonna.

3

1

*uido Reni: Slaughter of the Innocents. 2. Giovanni Fran-
o Barbieri, called Guercino: St. Sebastian ministered by
e. 3. Annibale Carracci: The toilet of Venus. 4. France-
Mazzola, called Parmigianino: Madonna of St. Mar-
th's.*

4

ple suggest, from Cento Trasende, that is One Hundred Windows.

Collegio Illirico-Ungarico (Croatian and Hungarian College), today's **Collegio Venturoli** (n. 4), was renewed at the beginning of the 18th century by Giuseppe A. Torri. It still shows in the refectory the frescoes by Gioacchino Pizzoli, illustrating stories of *Croatian and Hungarian history* and the *lives of the most important National patron saints*. Originally, this institute housed the Hungarian students attending classes at Bologna University. Later on, according to the bequest of architect Angelo Venturoli, it became a charitable institution for needy boys, gifted for the Arts.

Palazzo Bentivoglio (n. 8), built in the mid-16th century and allegedly attributed to Ba-

---

1. Giuseppe M. Crespi: The farmstead. 2. Giuseppe Crespi: Portrait of a girl with a cat. 3. Bentivoglio Pal. 16th century. 4. Basilica of S. Martino: the 1879 façad

162

4

olomeo Triachini, shows a grand façade, on
three tiers, in which the experiences carried out
n the contemporary Roman palaces were filtered
through the Bologna taste. Also the inner court-
ard, perhaps designed by Domenico Tibaldi,
although incomplete, shows the main elements
f a far-reaching project, well-worth the atten-
on it drew from the local Arts' circles.

BASILICA DI S. MARTINO

Around the mid-13th century, a Carmelite
ommunity established itself in the now-
estroyed church of St. Niccolò near the Mar-
et Field. In 1272 the community moved to St.
Martin's, where a small church, which the Ord-
 soon decided to enlarge, had already existed
 least since 1217.

This project was not, however, carried out un-
l 1308 and in 1315 it had to be interrupted for
e opposition of the Augustinian Brothers of St.
ames's who could hardly tolerate the building

of another church so close to theirs. This obsta-
cle was soon removed with the help of the Free-
Town's Council and the works were therefore
completed by the the mid-century.

However, about a century later the work-site
was opened up again and, under the direction of
Giovanni da Brensa, new vaults were added to
the church (1457) while a span towards the entrance and a new façade were added between
1491 and 1496.

In 1504 the square in front of the church was
opened by razing a group of old houses which
had stood there and finally the church was consecrated in 1511.

The façade was remade in 1879 in «Gothic»
style according to a design by Giuseppe Modone-
si; the side door, instead, dates back to the 16th
century and presents in the lunette an epic terracotta relief by Francesco Manzini (1531), *St.
Martin Covering the Poor Man*.

In the church's inside, we can see in the first
left span the beautiful Paltroni chapel, square-
shaped in serene and pellucid Renaissance lines,
which had already been completed in 1506 when
the famous jurist and University lecturer of canon and civil law Alessandro Paltroni was buried
there. Around that same year, Francesco Raibolini, called «Francia», painted the charming *Enthroned Virgin with Child between Angels and
Saints*, the *Deposition* and *Christ Carrying the
Cross* which are found in the elegant frame made
by Formigine and below the *St. Roch* in the upper small window. The livid-coloured *Burial of
Christ* in the altar's front is by Amico Aspertini
and the fragment of a fresco with a *Nativity of
Christ*, recently found in the sacristy under layers of paint and placed here on the right wall,

163

2

1. The harmoniously Gothi
inside (14th-15th centuries). 2
Paolo Uccello: Christ's Nativ
ity. 3. St. Roch, a stained-glas
window by Giacomo da Ulm
from a drawing by Francia. 4
Vitale da Bologna: fragment o
a fresco with a Crucifix. 5
Francia: Madonna with Chil
and Saints.

4

the *Enthroned Virgin and Saints* was painted by Girolamo Sicciolante from Sermoneta in 1548. The organ is a precious instrument made by Giovanni Cipri from Ferrara (1556).

The small chapel of the *Madonna of Carmine* is quite lovely: it was built in 1752 according to the design of Alfonso Torreggiani and includes frescoes by Vittorio Bigari and a beautiful canvas portraying the *Saints Charles, Albert, Theresa and Francesca Romana* by Tiarini (ca. 1618).

If we walk down the church again along the right aisle, just after the first altar, we can see a *Virgin with Child between the Saints Lucia, Ambrogio, Nicola and Three Young Girls*, a masterpiece by the original, restless and moody painter Amico Aspertini, who often carried his eccentricity to the verge of irreverence (ca. 1515).

The last altar was decorated between 1523 and 1532 for the Boncompagni noble family (of which the reformer of the calendar, Pope Gregory XIII, born in 1502, was also a member).

Alessandro Bigli from Bergamo carved, according to the design of Bartolomeo da Bagnacavallo, the elegant wooden frame in which the wondrous *Adoration of the Kings* by Girolamo da Carpi (1501-1568) was later placed. The sandstone decorations were made by Bernardino di Cristoforo from Milan.

The column of the Madonna of Carmine, placed in a corner of the square in front of the church, was raised in 1705 according to the design of Architect Giovan Antonio Conti; the statue is by Andrea Ferreri.

by Paolo Uccello (Florence 1397-1475). The beautiful terracotta statue of the *Madonna of Carmine*, placed on the left wall, dates certainly back to the 15th century.

On the fourth altar we can see the restless painting of *St. Jerome* bathed in sunset's light by Ludovico Carracci (1555-1619), and on the fifth one the *Assumption of the Virgin* and the above lunette are by Lorenzo Costa (1506).

The splendid altar-piece on the high-altar with

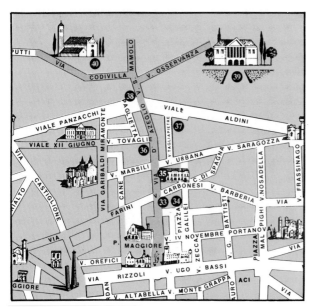

Via d'Azeglio

The street section which from piazza Maggiore leads to the gate demolished at the beginning of the 20th century, was called via San Mamolo, or San Mamante according to the popular usage. The new name was given in 1874. The old via San Mamolo was a large street; in fact, in the 18th century the passage of carriages was allowed along this street so as to reach the surrounding hills.

Corte dei Galluzzi is articulated in two communicating adjacent courtyards: the houses that once belonged to the Galluzzi family, including a 13th-century tower look into the one leading to via D'Azeglio while the other courtyard, reached through piazza Galvani, was called, up to the 19th century, «Pavaiuncin», that is «small Pavaglione». The **Pavaglione** was that area located behind the church of St. Petronius, today's piazza Galvani, where the «fiera dei foliselli», that is the silk-worms' fair, had been held since 1449. This ancient toponomy is still applied because the people of Bologna still call today's via dell'Archiginnasio with the ancient name of Pavaglione. Along via d'Azeglio we come across the **Chiesa di S. Giovanni Battista dei Celestini** (St. John the Baptist's Church of the Celestinian Brothers). The first church with a small adjacent monastery was built here in 1369 for the nobleman Antonio Galluzzi to house the small group of Celestinian Brothers who had come to Bologna the previous year.

During the 16th century, the Celestinian Brothers had the church completely restructured by starting the work from the main chapel, wholly changed and enlarged between 1520 and 1523, and terminating them in 1595 with the raising of the bell-tower. The works were directed at fir by Lorenzo di Pietro Tassi and continued, afte his death (1552), by Bartolomeo di Antonio Ta si, both of them called «Triachino». After th death of Bartolomeo in 1587, the works wer taken up by Architect Tommaso Martelli.

The church's façades and the adjacen monastery (today's the State Archives) wer raised only in 1770 following a design by A chitect Francesco Tadolini.

The church's inside, so elegantly and preciou ly elaborated, was strongly affected by the gene al decoration works carried out between 1687 an 1727. The works started with the main chape (1687-88), on whose vault Giovanni Antonio Bu rini, for the figures, and Enrico Haffner, for th decorations, represented the *Glory of St. Pie Celestino*; Antonio Orsoni carved the imposin wooden frame; Giuseppe Mazza moulded *Faith Meekness and Putti with the Symbol of the Celes tinian Brothers* in the cyma, and the two expres sive busts of *St. Benedict* and *St. Scholastica* once placed at both sides of the altar-piece an today in the two niches at the sides of the mai church door; finally, Marcantonio Franceschir painted the beautiful altar-piece with the *En throned Virgin with Child between the Saint John the Baptist, Pier Celestino and Luke*.

In 1714, the painters Giacomo Boni and Gia

---

1. Church of S. Giovanni Battista dei Celestini: the 1770 f çade. 2 and 3. State Archives: 17th-century miniature fr the Elders' «Insignia».

2

3

ito Garofalini, for the figures, and Luca Biste-
, for the decorations, painted the nave's vaults
th: the *Offer of the Pope's Tiara to the Her-
it Pietro da Morrone*; *Pier Celestino, In-
duced by Meekness, Places the Tiara at the
et of Religion*; and finally, the *Death of the
int*.

Let us mention, among the many artworks to
found in the church and adjacent premises,
e following: the altar-piece with *St. Sebastian
d St. Irene* on the first altar to the left, a work
inted by Andrea Donducci, also called
Mastelletta» (1575-1655), when he was very old;
e magnificent *Noli Me Tangere* by Lucio Mas-
ri (1569-1633); the *Virgin Appearing to St. Pier
elestino in a Dream* by Emilio Taruffi, placed
the baptistry face-to-face the *Virgin of Pup-
's*, a Renaissance wooden sculpture of North-
n inspiration; the panel *St. John the Baptist*,
rt of a dismembered polyptych by Francesco
ganelli (1513) in the parish's office; and final-
, the elegant sacristy room, decorated in 1776
cording to a design by Francesco Tadolini.

The large monastery, in piazza de' Celestini 4,
jacent to the church of St. John the Baptist
tes back to 1369 but was completely restruc-
red by Carlo Francesco Dotti, who built the
y *main cloister* between 1729 and 1754. The
th-century façade is by Francesco Tadolini.
nce 1940 it has housed the important **State Ar-
ives**, which were permanently placed there in
e 60's. The Archives, with documents dating
om the 10th to the 20th centuries, are divided
into several sections: *City-State's archives*
2th-15th centuries), *Pontifical archives*
6th-18th centuries), *archives of «autonomous*

bodies» (19th century: comprising the Napoleonic period, the Legations' period, the Provisional
Government of the Romagne), the *archives of the
suppressed convents* (12th-18th centuries). The
collection of about 2,000 seals starting from the
13th century is quite valuable as well as the
library founded in 1874.

*The State Archives are open for consultation from
Monday to Friday from 8.30 a.m. to 7 p.m.; on Saturdays from 8.30 a.m. to 1.30 p.m. They are closed on
holidays.*

Palazzo Legnani (n. 38), originally from the
16th century, was rebuilt in 1870 by Antonio
Zannoni. Inside, there are a 19th-century grand
staircase by Gabriele Chelini, two centaurs in the
courtyards and the sculptures by Petronio Tadolini (1758), representing *Hercules* and two figures
symbolising two rivers.

In the inner courtyard of the **former Casa dei
Carbonesi** (n. 27) we can admire a front styled
as a Neoclassical temple.

Casa Mezzovillani (n. 42) and **Casa Rizzi** (n.
35) are very evocative in their inner courtyards
with 15th-century decorations.

Palazzo Sanuti, today's **Bevilacqua** palace (ns.
31-33), raised in 1477 by Tuscan masons and
renewed in its inside by Galeazzo Alessi in 1531,
is characterized by at least three elements which
are foreign to the Renaissance culture in Bolo-

gna, that is the lack of an arcade, the absence of a cotto facing, replaced instead by the grey-coloured sandstone of the Porretta quarries, enhanced by the particularly chromatic effect of the ashlar works, and finally the nitidly perspective effect given by the horizontal cornices and skirt roofing. The inner courtyard is characterized by two tiers of superimposed small open galleries; some architectural elements, such as the pulvins crowning the Corinthian capitals or the use of a high entablature, push upwards the square-shaped arcade. Historical documents, mentioned by 18th-century authors from Bologna, seem to attest to the intervention of Donato Bramante in the remodelling of this palace.

In **Palazzo Marsigli** (n. 48) it is still possible to see the high-rise section originally belonging to the observatory built for Count Luigi Ferdinando Marsigli by the master mason G. A. Taruffi (1702) in order for the count to carry out his astronomical studies. The inner courtyard is characterized by the scenic effect of a balcony planned by Carlo Francesco Dotti.

CHIESA DI SAN PROCOLO

This church is one of the oldest seats of t Benedictine order established in Bologna.

The present church was built around t mid-11th century on the tomb of St. Procolu one of the first martyrs for the faith of the loc Christian community. From the 12th century o ward, it became the meeting place for the Unive sity's student organizations, so as to be called t «cradle of the University» (Fliche - Martin).

Martinus and Bulgarus, the two famo Masters at Law called together with Jacopo a Ugo by the Emperor Frederick Barbarossa to a tend the Roncaglia Diet, held near Piacenza November 1158, in order to firmly attest the E peror's supremacy on the recalcitrant Itali Free-Towns, were buried on the parvis of the S Proculus's church, thus stressing its early affir ty and link with the University. Between 1383 a 1407, thanks to the action of the Benedictine a bot Giovanni di Michele, the church saw the ra ing of its serene-looking Gothic façade and cross-vaults over the nave and aisles.

1. Sanuti Bevilacqua Palace, 1477, one of the first witho arcades. 2. The magnificently carved portal, set in the ash front in hard sand-stone. 3. Church of S. Procolo, with lovely terracotta portal (14th century).

During general remodelling works carried out by Architect Antonio Morandi, also called «Terribilia», around the mid-16th century, the vaults were changed, the church was lenghtened by adding another span and the massive bell-tower was built. Architect Domenico Tibaldi built the large round choir, which was later raised and remodelled by Architect Carlo Francesco Dotti in 1744.

The façade has a fine 14th-century portal and, in the nearby wall, a small plaque is to be found inscribed with the well-known Latin play on words: SI PROCUL A PROCULO PROCULI CAMPANA FUISSET NUNC PROCUL A PROCULO PROCULUS IPSE FORET (the date 1393 was mistakenly reported during a trancription) which means: «If Proculus had been away from the Proculus's bell, now Proculus would be away from Proculus», thus referring to the sad story of Proculus della Maglia, the church's bell-ringer, who died in 1538 when a section of the bell-tower collapsed and was, therefore, buried next to the bell-tower's basement.

The church contains several artworks of great interest. The second chapel on the left, *dedicated to St. Proculus* and completely rebuilt in 1741 according to a design by Alfonso Torreggiani (1682-1764), has an altar-piece by Francesco l'Ange (1675-1756) and two ovals by Carlo Cesare Giovannini (ca. 1695-1758). The sumptuous high altar decorated with valuable marble and semi-precious stones was built in 1752 according to a design by Torreggiani. Its marble ornament is by the Toselli brothers and the bronzes by Bonaventura Gambari. The *ark of St. Proculus*, a late-Roman marble work turned into a Christian tomb, is placed behind the altar.

An *Adoration of the Kings*, a peculiar blend of painting, relief and carving, by Bartolomeo Cesi (1556-1629), who had here also his family chapel and also painted the uplifting *St. Benedict in Ecstasy* in the second chapel on the right, is placed in a niche under the organ, a precious instrument by Baldassarre Malamini (1580).

The nearby former Benedictine monastery of St. Proculus, today's the Newborn Ward of the Main Hospital «C. A. Pizzardi» still contains three well-preserved cloisters: the cloister *of the Chapter* or *of the Gate* built by Giulio Dalla Torre on a design by Domenico Tibaldi in 1586; the one *of the Sacristy* raised by Giulio Dalla Torre between 1612 and 1628; the *Refectory* one, built by the brothers Giacomo and Benedetto Dalla Torre in 1548, who applied architectural lines similar to the ones found in cloisters from Ferrara; and finally a courtyard with a monumental arcade raised by Giulio Dalla Torre between 1573 and 1584 and which recalls similar works by Terribilia.

Chiesa del Corpus Domini or **della Santa** (via Tagliapietre, 10). On 13th November 1456 a group of Poor Clare nuns, who had come to Bologna from Ferrara just four months before,

took possession, under the guide of St. Cathe-
ine de' Vigri, of the old monastery of S
Christopher which was located on the corner be
tween the present via Urbana and Via Bocca c
Lupo and, in a few years' time, it came to in
clude the whole block, thanks to donations an
acquisitions.

Between 1477 and 1480, the nuns had their in
ner church (for the cloistered sisters) bui
together with the public one of Corpus Domin
raised by the master-builders Nicolò di Ma
chionne from Florence and Francesco Fucci fron
Dozza. The serene Renaissance cotto façade wa
made by an unknown but able master modeller
perhaps Sperandio from Mantua who was activ
in those years in Bologna, but who could proba
bly be identified in one of the best followers o
Pagno di Lapo or Antonio di Simone, both fron
Florence, for the evident Tuscan features in th
decoration.

Between 1684 and 1695 Architect Gian Giaco
mo Monti directed the remodelling of the church
without touching the façade, he managed t
lengthen it by about three metres by moving bac
the end wall to the detriment of the inner church
He also built the big side chapels and made th

*1. Church of Corpus Domini (15th-17th centuries). 2. Th
magnificent terracotta portal from the end of the 15th cen
tury. 3. The uncorrupted body of St. Catherine of Bologne
4. Marcantonio Franceschini: The death of St. Joseph.
Church of SS. Annunziata (15th century).*

munion of the Apostles, a painting by Franceschini and by the complex decorative work with the *Eternal Father in Glory* and the *Saints Francis and Clare* by Mazza who also made all the statues and the reliefs in the nearby chapel, dedicated to the Virgin of the Rosary. In this chapel we can admire two beautiful canvasses, placed on the sides, by Ludovico Carracci: the *Descent of Christ in Limbo* and the *Assumption of the Virgin*.

In the next small chapel, we can see the tomb of the famous physician Luigi Galvani, who first carried out studies on electric physiology, and, at the centre of the church's floor, the tomb of Laura Bassi Veratti, teacher of experimental physics at the Institute of Sciences and rare example of a woman-scientist who lived in the 18th century.

On the last altar, we can see the valuable *St. Francis* by Denjs Calvaert (1540-1619).

If we turn left after leaving the church, we can reach through a carriage gateway the *old cloister* (1461) with its beautifully-modelled cotto capitals.

The **Confraternita degli Innocenti** (via d'Azeglio ns. 41-43) was a 16th-century institute for abandoned children; now a section of this building is occupied by the Soffitta Theatre (n. 41).

Il **Palazzo del Collegio Montalto**, today's **Collegio San Luigi** (n. 55) was planned by Pietro Fiorini (1586) in order to house there the University's students from the Marches. It was later enlarged by Francesco Guerra.

Just after porta S. Mamolo, you will find the group of church and monastery of the **SS. Annunziata**, even today partly occupied by military installations and barracks. The building of the church was started in 1488 on the exact location where once had stood the monastery of the Basilian Brothers and was commissioned by the Franciscan Brothers. The church's front is provided with an arcade which was frescoed in 1619 with the *Tales of the Virgin Mary*; the church has one nave and two aisles in Gothic-

church higher, thus making it more spacious and luminous. As the construction proceeded, the decorative artists started also their work, and in a few years the artists engaged, Marco Antonio Franceschini for the figures, Enrico Haffner for the painted ornament, and Giuseppe Mazza for the plastic decoration, created a place of rarely-found magnificence.

Unfortunately, almost everything was reduced to dust in just a few seconds by bombs during an air raid on 5th October 1943.

The church's inside shows now, on the first altar to the left, the famous, much seen and copied, oval by Franceschini (1692), portraying the *Death of St. Joseph*.

From the second altar (right door) we can reach the small chapel, dedicated to St. Catherine from Bologna, whose body, still intact, is kept there. This Saint, who had founded the Monastery, was a contemplative hermit, an amateur painter and musician. In the chapel, which survived the bombing, Mazza worked in the stucco decoration, Franceschini in the figures, together with Luigi Quaini, and Haffner in the decoration. The work was completed in just 25 days (June 1687).

The adjacent room hosts a small, interesting Museum of memoirs and items from the monastery and its founder, whom the Bolognese call *the Saint*.

The high altar is dominated by the giant *Com-*

5

Renaissance style whereas its apse dates back to 1620. In 1687-90, the nice bell-tower was rebuilt by Giovanni Battista Della Casa. This group was completely transformed in the inside during the Baroque period, and suffered further damage when it became a military post in 1870. The church, since its re-establishment in 1944, has been subjected to many restoration campaigns in order to bring back its pristine late 15th-century features. In one section of the monastery, still today's Army's property, the detached department of artillery has its office, which includes also the **Museo delle armi e delle munizioni «Pietro Comito»** (Museum of Weapons and Ammunitions).

The museum is open to the public on 4th November; on all the other days, a visit is possible previous request at the Headquarters of the Military District (via Galliera 1, tel. 232095-237613).

The second side street on the right is **Via dell'Osservanza**. This street's layout was first set by Paolo Canali in 1659-60. Fourteen small piers mark the stations of an 18th-century *Way of the Cross*, whose terracotta statues were modelled by Gaetano Pignoni. The Neoclassical **Villa Aldini** was built by Giuseppe Nadi and Giovan Battista Martinetti at the top of the Osservanza hill for Antonio Aldini, minister of Napoleon Bonaparte. The older shrine of the Madonna of the Hill (12th century) was included in the villa's plan, and its Romanesque round terrace became a dining or music room. The villa's front, in Ionian style, bears a stucco relief by Giacomo De Maria, representing the Olympus, on the tympanum. The frescoes dating from the 12th century (*Madonna* and *Apostles*) are found in the Romanesque *Rotunda*. The nearby church of *S. Paolo in Monte*, built by the Franciscans, also called of the «Osservanza», at the end of the 15th century, was renewed along to Neoclassical lines by Vincenzo Vannini in 1828.

1. Neoclassic Villa Aldini includes also the Romanesque Rotunda of the Madonna del Monte. 2. Church of S. Paolo in Monte at the Osservanza (19th century). 3. The large S. Michele in Bosco's church compound dominating the town.

AN MICHELE IN BOSCO

The hospital and monastery group of the Rizoli Orthopaedic Institute, located in the former livetan convent, with an entrance in via Giulio esare Pupilli 2 and another in the piazzale S. Iichele in Bosco, stand on the hill once called elvedere.

Chiesa di S. Michele in Bosco. Already in 1114 as a small religious community living up here. e do not know much about it, only that all its embers died during the Black Death of 1348. Owing to that tragic event, the cardinal legate ndroino della Rocca assigned that place to the livetan Benedictine order in 1364. However, the others were to be forced out of their church several occasions by battles and war, which is iderstandable given the strategic importance of at hill for those who wanted to defend or con-er the town. Nevertheless, they always anaged to come back. The church was des-oyed and rebuilt many times until its final and rmanent reconstruction, carried out between 17 and 1523, by adapting perhaps a design by e great architect from Ferrara, Biagio Rossetti . 1516). The marble portal, carved by Giaco-o of Andrea da Formigine and Bernardino da ilano in 1522 according to a design by the great chitect Baldassarre Peruzzi from Siena, stands it from the beautiful terracotta façade for its assicly-elaborated lines, its refined execution d the chromatic effect of the material used. ie side portal is to be attributed to Andrea da rmigine (1525).

The elegant bell-tower, built in 1520 and modelled in 1788, had its cusp cut off on 1862. was rebuilt in 1890.

The church has a single-nave plan and still keeps intact, lengthwise, the traditional separation between the monks' church (here, at a higher level) and the one of the faithful (at a lower level).

The giant organ, a precious instrument made by Giovan Battista Facchetti from Brescia in 1509 (the classical decorative elements in the sound-box were added in 1526) towers over the entrance.

By walking from left to right in the faithful's church, we can find: over the side doors *four ovals held by charming putti*, a lively youthful work by Carlo Cignani (1628-1719); the chapel dedicated to *St. Francesca Romana* with the Saint's image by Alessandro Tiarini (1577-1668), the fresco decoration (*Glory of the Saint and Tales of her Life*) by Gioacchino Pizzoli (1705), and the tomb of Francesco Rizzoli, the founder of the Rizzoli Orthopaedic Institute, whose fame is reknown throughout the world. In the small facing chapel, the canvas portraying the *Passage of St. Carlo Borromeo* and the frescoed *Tales* of his life were painted by Tiarini in 1614.

The two side confessionals were carved with masterly workmanship in 1521 by Raffaele da Brescia, who had worked also in the stalls in the choir, which was unfortunately destroyed in the last century; some remaining inlay from that choir are to be found today in the Holy Sacrament chapel in St. Petronius's.

Finally, the *tomb of Armaciotto de' Ramazzotti* built between 1525 and 1526 by Alfonso Lombardi for the figures and by Bernardino da Milano for the decoration is placed under the chancel. The latter artist made also the charming nearby holy water stoup in 1534. The monks' church can be reached by following the stairs flanked by statues portraying *King David, the prophet Isaiah and the saints Benedict and Mauro*, made by Giovanni Maria Rossi in 1662.

The main chapel's arch was carved by Ber-

nardino da Milano (ca. 1525); the frescoes over the arch (the *Archangel Michael Chasing the Devils*) as well as the one on the dome and in the vault are by Domenico Canuti (1620-1684).

The marble and semi-precious stones tabernacle made by Giovanni da Piacenza in 1619 is quite outstanding. The altar-piece is a copy (by Federico Gnudi, 1850) of the painting by Innocenzo da Imola (1494-1550) moved to the Picture Gallery. The nearby sacristy (on the left) is also quite beautiful. On its back wall, Bartolomeo Ramenghi from Bagnacavallo (1484-1542) frescoed the *Transfiguration*, imitating the famous painting by Raphael. The small chapel contains very lively frescoes by fra Paolo Novello d'Arpino (1622); the other frescoes were painted by Girolamo da Carpi (the side walls), Biagio Pupini and Girolamo Borghese (the ceiling) in 1525.

By going back into the church, in front of the sacristy we can find two doors leading to the octagonal cloister, the bigger one, and to the monastery, the smaller.

1. Church of S. Michele in Bosco, 16th century. 2. The church's rich inside, decorated in the 16th-17th centuries. 3. Alfonso Lombardi: tomb of Armaciotto de' Ramazzotti. 4. Bagnacavallo: Transfiguration.

3

175

The octagonal cloister, an enchantingly evocative place, was built between 1602 and 1603 according to a design by Architect Pietro Fiorini and decorated, just in the next few years, by Ludovico Carracci and his students (Tiarini, Reni, Cavedoni, Spada, Massari and others) with the tales of St. Benedict, and the tales of St. Cecilia and St. Valerianus, a well-famous series of frescoes, now unfortunately almost completely ruined.

By going through the monastery's door we can find first the night choir frescoed by Innocenzo da Imola in 1517, then the tombstones of the jurist Antonio da Budrio by Jacopo della Quercia (1435) and of the other master at law Egidio di Lobia (1319), and finally we reach the long corridor looked into by the monks' cells, the longest enclosed space in Bologna (162.25 metres), on whose floor the lengths of all the other important town's buildings are marked. A peculiar perspective effect takes place in here: as we move away from the large window (the view is quite breathtaking), the Asinelli tower, framed by that same window, seems to become bigger instead of decreasing.

Since 1896, S. Michele in Bosco has been the seat of the **Orthopaedic Institute Rizzoli**, established in 1880 thanks to the considerable bequest made by the surgeon Francesco Rizzoli, and famous throughout the world. The collections of the **Donation of the Surgeon Vittorio Putti** (1880-1940) are displayed in the old refectory of

the brothers and in their library. The former refectory, frescoed by Vasari and his students, with a large painting by the master painter from Arezzo *Jesus in the House of Martha* (1539), is now the seat of the *Collection of Surgical Instruments* from all periods, from the decline of the Roman Empire to the 19th and 20th centuries. This collection includes also the instruments and equipment of Cesare Tartùferi, Francesco Rizzoli and Alessandro Codivilla (two ivory *anatomical dummies* from the 17th and 18th centuries). The collection of medals from the 16th to the 19th centuries is also very valuable as is interesting the portrait gallery. The magnificent *library of the brothers*, in which the *Library Umberto I* is located, was built by Giovan Giacomo Monti in 1677-80 and frescoed by Domenico Maria Canuti and Enrico Haffner during those same years. The Library, set up in 1920, comprises 16,000 volumes, including 1,158 important medicine and surgery text-books dating back to the 14th to the 18th centuries (including 17 manuscripts, 66 incunabula, and 238 books print-

---

1. Pietro Fiorini: octagonal cloister (1602-1603). 2. 18th-century clock in the vast corridor. 3. Monastery of S. Vittore: the cloister (15th century).

d during the 16th century). A *globe* by Matteo Greuter and an *armillary sphere* (1528) by Gerolamo della Volpaia are placed in the hall.

The Rizzoli collections can be visited from Monday to Friday from 10.30 a.m. to 1.30 p.m.; on Saturdays from 9 a.m. to 1 p.m.; they are close on Holidays. Tel. 6366111

CHIESA DI S. VITTORE

The first documented information regarding cloister on the St. Vittore hill dates back to 1062 and of that early building nothing remains but small chapel, remodelled into the square apse of today's church. The nave was raised in the following century and the church was consecrated by the bishop of Bologna, Giovanni V, in 1178, to be used by the regular Canons.

After the church's suppression during the Napoleonic period and calamitous times of neglect, the church was bought in 1830 by the Oratorian Brothers of St. Filippo Neri, who started its restoration. However, they had to abandon it into the hands of the Corps of Engineers in 1860; in 1892 the restoration works could be started up again and now the church is again open to public worship.

The church is one of the few oldest churches in Bologna to have kept unchanged the traditionally strict separation between the section for the worshippers and the one for the monks (chancel), achieved here through a sturdy wall, pierced above by a Romanesque small open gallery very elegantly supported by six arches at whose centre, on the choir's direction, the ancient image of St. Vittore (13th century) is frescoed, and below by a small door.

In the worshippers' church there is an ark in which the remains of the bishop of Bologna, Enrico della Fratta, who died in 1241, were placed and in the monks' church there is an old wooden choir built by Pellegrino degli Anselmi from Bologna and Pietro di Antonio from Florence.

The altar is a modern copy of the one that is to be found at the centre of the church of S. Giovanni in Monte. The airy cloister is the result of the 15th-century remodelling of a 12th-century cloister of which almost all the marble pilasters have survived.

The well dates back to 1560. The plaques along the inner walls of the cloister recall the historical events of the monastery and the famous people who have stopped, lived and died there, such as Ugo di Porta Ravegnana, famous jurist, one of the four masters at law invited by Frederick Barbarossa to participate in the Roncaglia Diet (1158) on the supremacy of the Emperor's rights.

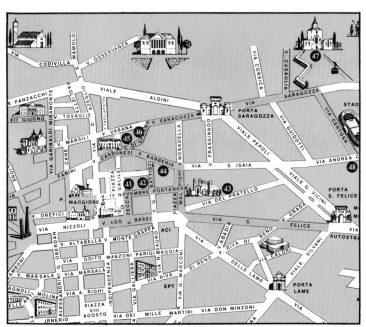

Via Ugo Bassi

Via Ugo Bassi was completely rebuilt in the 1920's and 30's, when the strong concentration of an increased traffic made circulation impossible in the old street's layout. In fact, the previous via dei Vetturini, made for horse-drawn carts and buggies, was only six-metres large.

The area of the Palazzo Pubblico's (Municipal Palace) courtyard, where in 1568 the Botanical Garden, or Garden of the Simple, set up by the famous naturalist Ulisse Aldrovandi, was placed, is now occupied by the building in which the Stock Market had its seat in 1886. The so-called **Old Fountain**, a work by Giovanni Andrea della Porta according to a design by Tommaso Laureti, was placed in this building's front. Let us observe the fountain's ashlar-work facing, the break in the curved pediment so as to include the coat of arms and the cusp crowning.

Palazzo della Dogana (Customs' palace at n. 1), today's the seat of the Banco di Roma bank, was planned by Domenico Tibaldi, but the original project was later changed in the front by Angelo Venturoli. The fact that on the opposite side once stood the Mint Palace, razed in order to carry out the 1889 town's planning scheme, further stresses the important role played by this street in the economic life of the town in the 16th century. It was a time during which the town's planning was aimed at concentrating in the same area all the public buildings, thereby linking the symbols of the political and religious power, in order to further control the town's cultural life and wealth, basically tradeable goods. By taking a left-hand side street, so as to continue on the west side of the Palazzo Pubblico, we rea **Palazzo Caprara** in via IV Novembre ns. 22-2 today's the seat of the PREFECTURE (Provi cial Administration), remodelled in 1732 by A fonso Torreggiani. The courtyard was built Giuseppe Antonio Torri, to whom the grai staircase and the two facing flights are also to attributed. In the reception apartment, twel tempera paintings on canvas, representing lan scapes dotted with ruins, by Mirandolese are be seen over the doors.

In the 17th-century **Palazzo dall'Armi** (n. ! seat of the NATIONAL OFFICE FOR TH PROTECTION OF CULTURAL AND A CHITECTURAL HERITAGE, we can admi wall paintings by artists from Bologna from t

1. Via Ugo Bassi, from the west. 2. Roosevelt Square: on t right, Caprara Palace. 3. Caprara Palace: the grand stairc by Torri.

178

Ith and 18th centuries, and in particular the *Allegory of Air and Fire* by Guido Reni and an elliptical room decorated by Giani.

In via Cesare Battisti, the fourth side street on the left of via Ugo Bassi, it is possible to see further examples of 15th-century houses, all with courtyards: **Palazzo Garagnani** (n. 7), **Pandolfi** (n. 13), **Desideri** (n. 22) and **Felicini** (n. 23).

CHIESA DEL SS. SALVATORE

The Regular Canons of St. Mary of Reno had their seat in here since 1136. They were a community of priests who, having embraced the rule of St. Augustine and the decrees of the 1059 Lateran Synod, decided not only to live together in poverty but also to place a greater attention on pastoral activity and to the achievement of an ideal of charity and love which were given somehow less attention by monks striving for personal perfection. The old small church of the canons, whose early origin was allegedly dated from 1056, was remodelled at the end of the 15th century but was later on completely erased by the new church, built on a grand scale by Vincenzo Porta according to a design by architects Ambrogio Mazenta, a Barnabite brother, and Tommaso Martelli between 1606 and 1623. The church's sides are imposing, its façade, built on classic features, is serene and noble-looking. It is decorated and embellished by four terracotta statues (1615-1622), once painted to look like bronze, portraying the *Evangelists* by Giovanni Tedeschi and crowned by the giant copper statues, once gilded, made by Orazio Provaglia during those same years.

The inside is magnificent. In the first chapel on the right, the altar-piece with *St. Giovanni-*

no, St. Zaccariah, St. Ann and Other Saints is by the excellent painter from Ferrara, Benvenuto Tisi, also called «Garofalo» (1542); in the second, the *Ascension* is by Carlo Bononi (1569-1632) while the side statues are by Giovanni Tedeschi (1622-24), the author, together with stucco-work decorative artist Andrea Guerra, of almost all the plastic decorations of the church, including the elegant inner façade. On the fourth altar the giant figures of the *Holy Family* are by Alessandro Tiarini (1577-1668). The main chapel is dominated by *Jesus the Saviour in Glory*, a work by Giovan Francesco Gessi helped by Gui-

do Reni, who had also designed it (1620). *Ki David* found above among the prophets is Giacomo Cavedoni (1577-1660) who painted al the canvas *The Infidels Fighting over the Beiro Crucifix*; the other painting with the *Baptism the Infidels* is by Francesco Brizzi (1574-162 The altar and the ciborium were carved on pr cious marble according to the design of Cami Ambrosi (1725-1790).

By going back towards the church's entran along the righ side, we come to the first lar; chapel which contains a precious polyptych Vitale da Bologna (1353) representing the *Crow ing of the Virgin Surrounded by the Nativi scene, the Martyrdom of St. Catherine and Seve al Saints. The Virgin at the temple with St. Th mas Becket*, placed in front of the polyptych, u

1. *Church of SS. Salvatore, 17th century. 2. Lippo (attr Madonna known as the «Victory» one. 3. Carlo Bono Christ's Ascent. 4. Porta Nova Arch frames the steeples S. Francesco's Church.*

r the choir, is by Girolamo da Treviso
508-1544). It was originally in the older church
er the altar of the English scholars (the saint
d studied in Bologna and probably had attend-
this church together with the other foreign stu-
nts).
The beautiful sacristy is decorated with good-
ality paintings, such as *The Saviour* by Cave-
ne, *David* by Giovan Antonio Burrini
556-1727) and *St. John the Baptist* by Giuseppe
aria Crespi, also called the «Spanish»
565-1747).
The *Madonna of the Victory*, a late 14th-
ntury panel, attributed to Lippo di Dalmasio,
ich was originally in the del Monte church (to-
y's villa Aldini), is placed on the second altar.
1 the next one, there is a large canvas by An-
ea Donducci, also called «Mastelletta»
575-1655), the *Resurrection of Christ*. The
tues above are by Clemente Molli, the ones be-
v by Tedeschi.
The saints frescoed over the arches of the
aller chapels are by Cavedoni. At the floor's
ntre you can see the tomb of Giovanni Fran-
sco Barbieri, also called «Guercino», the great
inter who was given hospitality by the Canons
nen he moved to Bologna from Cento and who
ιs buried here according to his will (1666).

4

Piazza Malpighi - Via S. Felice

An Ionic column, crowned by a statue of the
rgin, made by Giovanni Tedeschi in 1638,
nds in *Piazza Malpighi*, once called «selicia-
> of St. Francis from the church's dedication:
st in front of it we can glimpse at the defen-
e tower of **Porta Nova** from the 13th century
d belonging to the second ring of walls encom-
ssing the city. It is the only gate still sporting
e original selenite hinges on its doors.

ASILICA DI S. FRANCESCO

Bernardo di Quintavalle, one of the first dis-
les of Francis, reached Bologna in 1218 and
unded here at first a community of Friars
nor near the church of S. Maria delle Puglio-
(in today's via del Porto). A few years after-
rds, in 1222, the Saint from Assisi himself
ne to town where he preached in piazza Mag-
pre. The community grew rapidly in the num-
r of people and churches and in 1235 they were
owed to move here, outside the town's walls
e the defensive tower of Porta Nova in piazza
ιlpighi), where they began to build their
ιrch, by starting with the apse, completed in

1254, and continuing on up to the façade, which
ended the works in 1263.

The church, vast and arranged as a cathedral,
is one of the first Gothic places of worship ever
built in Italy. Pretty soon, meetings of the
University's Medicine and Art students started
to be held here and it was also chosen as the burial place of many masters of the Studium of
Bologna. In this regard, the three **tombs of the
Glossatori** (the masters at Roman law), located
behind the apse, are quite famous. From the left-
hand side we can see: the tomb of Accursius and
his son Francis, built around 1250; the one of
Odofredus, who died in 1265, and finally the one
of Rolandino de Romanzi, made in 1284 by Alberto di Guidobono and Albertino di Enrico.

The main bell-tower, characterized by more
mature and ornated Gothic features, is also quite
outstanding: it was built between 1397 and 1404
from a design by Antonio di Vincenzo, the architect of St. Petronius' church, while the more
modest nearby bell-tower, built for a single bell,
according to the Franciscan rules, dates back to
the 13th century as the imposing façade with a
rather simple hipped profile, of Romanesque influence, but embellished by typically Gothic

181

decoration as: the marble reliefs shaped as symbolic animals at the sides of the Venetian style main portal; the lancet windows and the rose-windows opening skyward on the sides of the nave.

The ceramic basins which decorate the high section, and which date back for the most part to the 13th century, are quite beautiful. The church, which was to be greatly embellished by a great number of monuments and artworks in the following five centuries, was strongly affected by tampering between 1798 and 1886 when, after being deconsecrated, was used as a Customs warehouse, a salt store-house, and a military depot. It was heavily and extensively restored later on by Alfonso Rubbiani but again was heavily damaged by bombings on 24th July and 25th September 1943. Therefore, although rebuilt soon afterwards by the Architect Alfredo Barbacci, it cannot fully show its real age but none the less it still fascinates for the imaginative display of its construction.

1. The slender verticality of the church's Gothic inside. 2. Malpighi Square, with the dynamic and imposing apse of S. Francesco's, the Glossatori's arks and the Immaculate's column.

Along the left aisle we can see the *variegated
terracotta tomb of Pope Alexander V* who died
in Bologna in 1410. The upper section is by Pietro
Lamberti (1424), the base by Sperandio from
Mantua (1482).

The altar-piece on the high-altar is an authentic masterpiece of Italy's Gothic sculpture, made
between 1388 and 1393 by the sculptors Jacobello

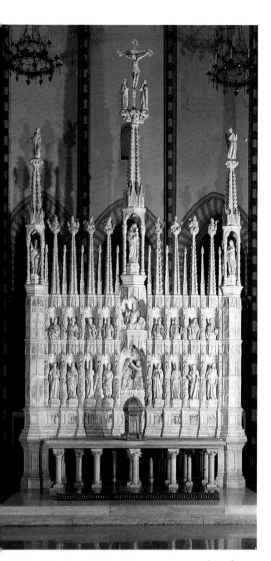

ceramics made by the Minghetti kilns and, in the fourth chapel to the left, two old sepulchres, the first one of *Vianesio Albergati the elder*, a refined work by Francesco di Simone Ferrucci from Fiesole (late 15th century), and the second of *Vianesio the younger*, a purely imitative work by Lazzaro Casario (16th century).

By walking down the church along the right aisle, we can admire the monumental *tomb of Alessandro Zambeccari* by Casario (1571), crowned by a cyma added in 1813 by Giacomo De Maria as a memento of the count Francesco Zambeccari, who had died the previous year in the fall of his aerostatic balloon.

At the end of the aisle, the *monument to the physician and philosopher Ludovico Boccadiferro*, who died in 1545, is placed above the church's side door. It was built by Girolamo Coltellini, perhaps following a design by Giulio Romano.

The *cloister of the dead* is also quite evocative: built along the south side of the church in the 13th century, it was remodelled in 1397. Several old tombstones of Bologna University's lecturers have been arranged there together with fragments of decorations removed from their original location during restoration works. The nearby *Muzzarelli Chapel*, now the sacristy, was built be-

d Pier Paolo Dalle Masegne, two brothers om Venice. In it they represented: in the predel- , the *Events of St. Francis's Life*, topped by the *owning of the Virgin* and by the *Eternal Father* nong hosts of *Saints*; on the spires, busts of *rophets*, the *Annunciation*, two *Angels Blowg Long Trumpets*, the *Virgin with Child* (add by Carlo Chelli from Carrara in 1884), and ally the *Crucifix* (a modern one) *between the rgin and St. John the Evangelist*.

In the apse's chapels, all decorated in the first ree decades of this century, we can admire: the ce flowery decoration of Achille Casanova; the

---

5

185

Nearby, in the arena of the now-buried Port of Bologna, is the *Salara (1785)*, a warehouse designed by Giuseppe Lanfranchini. Outside Porta Lame, the strips of land flanking the *Naviglio* or *Navile Canal* as far as the area of Corticella are involved in a gradual recovery project. It is planned first of all to restore this navigable waterway, essential to the Bolognese economy since the 12th century, when it joined the city to Malalbergo and the Po River. Since the Bentivoglio period (15th century), the Naviglio has been characterized by a system of basins with locks called supports, with doors by Leonardo da Vinci, reorganized by Vignola in the mid-16th century. A visit to the supports (*Bova, Battiferro, Torreggiani, Grassi, Landi, Corticella*) is highly interesting. A recovery, for new use, of the industrial archeological structures along th Naviglio has already begun. Thus, within th framework of a «Naviglio Park», a «scientifi and technological pole» of the University and th National Research Center will be established This will include the *House of innovation and in dustrial heritage*, in the ex-Gallotti Foundrie aimed at spreading awareness of the innovativ processes which have characterized production system in the Bologna area throughout history with its primary emphasis on activities such a the production and processing of silk, which al lowed Bologna to compete for centuries wit Lucca.

tween 1397 and 1400 according to a design by Antonio di Vincenzo.

By leaving through the back door, on piazza Malpighi, we can admire the lunettes all lined up underneath the arcade of the former Franciscan convent (today's the seat of the State Financial Bureau). They were frescoed by various painters during the 17th century and narrate events in the life of St. Anthony from Padua.

Most remarkable are the first lunettes from the right: the *Saint Enters the Convent to Don the Habit* by Alessandro Tiarini (1577-1668); the *Saint Donning the Habit* also by Tiarini; the *Saint Preaching to Franciscan and Dominican Brothers* by Angelo Michele Colonna (1600-1687). The tenth lunette is also quite interesting: it portrays the *Saint Forecasting Martyrdom to a Notary* by Giovan Battista Coriolano.

The deconsecrated **Chiesa di Santa Maria delle Laudi** (n. 1), facing the end of via U. Bassi, is attributed to Domenico Tibaldi; on its right side starts via S. Felice, which still has a few palaces remodelled in the 18th century, such as **Palazzo Ariosti** (n. 3), where Guido Reni was born, and **Palazzo Roffeni** (n. 21).

Palazzo Pallavicini (n. 26) is decorated with frescoes by Burrini (1690), which represent the *Tales of Phaeton and allegories of Felsina*.

The street ends with **Porta S. Felice**, rebuilt in 1506 and restored in 1805 for the visit of Napoleon I to the town. By continuing to the right, along the tree-lined avenues, we reach **Porta Lame**, planned by Agostino Barelli in 1676 according to the Baroque aesthetic taste. Next to the gate we can see the two bronze statues representing the *Partisans* by Luciano Minguzzi (1952).

1. Porta Lame, by Agostino Barelli (1676). 2.Via Barberia: S lina Brazzetti Palace (18th century).

Via Barberia

Via Barberia has kept its original denomination, although a change of name had been proposed at the end of the 19th century. In the old historical records of Bologna the street name was related to the societies or congregations established for the redeeming of the Barbary Coast's Christian slaves, but could also be referring, according to a more profane interpretation, to the races of Barbary horses, which were held there.

The original aristocratic feature, which had marked this street with their pride from the 16th to the 18th century, is still visible today in a few palaces built by architects of great renown. **Palazzo Marescotti** (n. 4), today's the seat of the Communist Party, dates back to the 16th century, as can be seen from its arcade decorated with interestingly shaped capitals. A grand two-flights staircase, designed (1680-1687) by Gian Giacomo Monti opens up inside, where there are many rooms decorated in the late-Baroque period, representing events relating to the Marescotti family: for example, on the salon ceiling Giuseppe and Antonio Rolli represented (1686-1687) the family's apotheosis while Giuseppe Antonio Caccioli painted on the walls the main political and social events, by also adding some allegorical and mythological tales.

In via Gombruti (the 4th side street to the right of via Barberia) we can find a building designed by Architect Alfonso Torreggiani (1756): **Palazzo Belloni** (n. 13), a quite large block of houses right in the town's centre, which comprises several buildings acquired by the family in various centuries. The palace, which is incomplete, this being a very uncommon event in the history of private dwellings in Bologna, lacks a homogeneity in its structure, due to its very long construction time, which made it pass as an heredity from fathers to sons. James III, the King of England, stayed in this palace with his entourage when visiting the town.

The heart of the Bolognese Jewish community, officially founded in 1911, is the building in via de' Gombruti 9: since 1829, Angelo Carpi of Cento had opened a Jewish oratorium here, and the Synagogue designed by the engineer Attilio Muggia was inaugurated on this site on 4 November 1928. The Israeli Temple, with its three naves and women's chapel, was destroyed by aerial bombs in 1943. It was rebuilt in 1954 by Guido Muggia, who re-interpreted his father's structure in modern style. The façde of the Synagogue, dominated by a rose window with the Star of David, looks out over the parallel street via Mario Finzi; here we find a memorial stone of the 83 Bolognese Jews deported in the winter of 1943, who never returned.

In via Barberia 13, the **Palazzo Salina Brazzetti** is a majestic and spectacular abode built by Carlo Francesco Dotti in 1720 for the Marquess Antonio Maria Monti Bedini. The façade was built also by Dotti in the years 1736-38. The inside was embellished with decorations by Ferdinando Bibiena and frescoes by Marcantonio Franceschini, Felice Cignani, Mariano Collina and others. The sculptures are by Giovanni Antonio Raimondi. *Palazzo Dondini* (n. 23) was on the place where once stood a ring of defensive towers; the faàde is to be attributed to Alfonso Torreggiani (1753), who decorated also the portals, one of which is false, with Rococo crownings. The staircase is by Gian Giacomo Dotti and the terrace-side garden, looking into piazza Malpighi planned by Fiorini in 1612, was once a riding-area.

Via de' Carbonesi: it is one of the most interesting archeological areas of the town. During the excavation seasons of 1982 and 1985 the *cavea of a Roman theatre* was found lying under the buildings of this block up to piazza de' Celestini. Through appropriate restoration works, the possibility of opening to visitors this important archeological find has been taken into consideration.

Palazzo Zambeccari (n. 11), the seat of the Banca Popolare of Milan, and built in 1775 by Carlo Bianconi, still maintains inside a valuable fresco, dedicated to Olympus, by Domenico Canuti and the decorative painter Giacomo Alboresi.

BASILICA DI S. PAOLO MAGGIORE

This church was started in 1606 by the regular clergy of St. Paul, known as «Barnabites» from the church of St. Barnabea in Milan, where they had established their first seat, and by 1611 the bearing structure was completed. The architect was a Barnabite, brother Ambrogio Mazenta from Milan (1565-1635) who applied here his concept of how a Counter-Reformation place of worship should be, that is vast, precious, airy, luminous, orderly and moderate.

The façade, commissioned by the Spada family, was raised between 1634 and 1636 according to the design of Architect Ercole Fichi who also modelled the terracotta statues of *St. Carlo Borromeo* and *St. Filippo Neri* for the upper niches. The marble statues of *St. Peter* and *St. Paul* were carved by Domenico Mirandola and finished by Giulio Cesare Conventi.

The inside is dominated by the splendid decoration in the vault, where *three scenes of St. Paul's life* were frescoed among large framing-works and imaginative architectural devices by the brothers Giuseppe Rolli, a figurative painter, and Antonio Rolli, a quadratura painter. When Antonio died in a fall from the scaffolding in 1696, his work was finished by Pier Antonio Guidi; the chapels, also, are full with invaluable artworks.

In the first chapel to the left we can see: the *Baptism of Christ* between the *Birth* and *Burial of St. John the Baptist*, three canvasses by Giacomo Cavedoni (1577-1660).

The third chapel, decorated in 1611, was one of the very first to be dedicated to St. Carlo Borromeo, canonized on 1st November 1610. The tragically expressive *St. Carlo Leading a Procession among the Plague Victims* and the two ashen-looking canvasses at its sides are by Lorenzo Barbieri (1588-1654). The dome (*St. Paul's*

Glory), the pendentives (*The Four Parts of the World*), the vaults of the transept and of the apse (*Conversion of St. Paul*, the *Saint Baptized by Ananias*, *St. Paul Destroying the Books of Sorcery*, *St. Paul in Prison*) were all painted, between 1716 and 1719, by Giuseppe Antonio Caccioli and Pier Francesco Farina, the same painters who decorated also the sacristy built by the architect Paolo Francesco Salteri in 1719.

The classically pellucid work by Donato Creti (1671-1749), *St. Alessandro Sauli* is to be found in the ante-sacristy. The massive high-altar was built between 1643 and 1650 thanks to the generosity of the Cardinals Francesco Borromini and Virgilio Spada. The Architect Francesco Borromini designed the altar table, the tabernacle and the magnificent marble backdrop. The Architect Domenico Facchetti designed the platform, characterized by nice features although its proportions are quite heavy. Alessandro Algardi (1595-1654) carved the medallion on the paliotto, the tabernacle's doors, the Crucifix (now stolen) and the important group of the *Beheading of St. Paul*. This work, made in Rome and sent to Bologna by sea, was captured by the pirates and had to be ransomed, thereby costing the considerable amount of 33,000 scudi. Above the altar of the right transept, we can find: *St. Gregorius Magnus and the Virgin Interceding for the Souls in the Purgatory*, a famous painting by Giovanni Francesco Barbieri, known as «Guercino» (1647) and the charming *Madonna of Providence (or Consolation)* by Filippo Dalmasio (1352-1410). The paintings above, at each side of the altar, together with the other two placed in front form a group portraying the *Creative, Redeeming, Natural and Adoptive Paternities of Christ*, a work by Giuseppe Maria Crespi

1665-1747). The perspective scenes painted by Angelo Maria Colonna (1600-1687) are also quite beautiful; the organ by Ottavio Negrelli (1647) is also of good quality.

By walking down the nave along the right side of the church, we can see in the first chapel the *Presentation of Christ to the Temple* by Aurelio Lomio, known as «Pisano» (1612) and, on the sides, the *Adoration of the Kings and the Shepherds*, one of the best works by Giacomo Cavedoni (1577-1660), who also frescoed the vault.

The second chapel has one of the most famous paintings by Ludovico Carracci (1555-1619); it represents the *Immaculate Conception of Mary* but it is known as the *Heavens* because the subject of the painting is more imagined than seen, through the hosts of saints and playing angels bathed in God's light.

In the last chapel, around a terracotta *Crucifix* modelled by Giovanni Tedeschi and painted by Francesco Albani in 1625, there are two beautiful canvasses representing the *Agony of Christ* and the *Calvary* made by Andrea Donducci, known as «Mastelletta» (1575-1665).

On the left side of the church of St. Paul starts via Collegio di Spagna, named after the Institute founded in 1365 by the Cardinal Egidio Albornoz to house the Spanish students attending classes at the University of Bologna. Planned by Matteo Giovannelli, also called Gattapone, the **Collegio di Spagna** (n. 4) is a functional two-storey build-

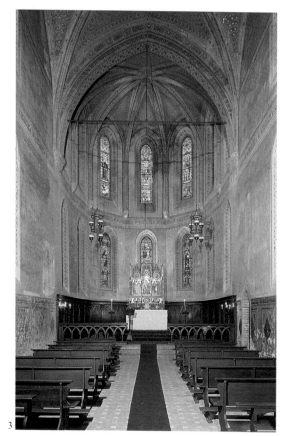

3

2

ing, with the rooms distributed along the arcaded courtyard in the centre. Encompassed by a crenellated wall, it has a valuable entrance portal made by Formigine (1525). It includes also the Gothic *Church of S. Clemente* (14th century) with a nice polyptych by Marco Zoppo (15th century).

By following the defensive wall of the college, we reach via Saragozza. Since the Middle Ages, the Albergati family had been living in this street: the magnificent **Palazzo Albergati** (ns. 26-28), attributed to Baldassarre Peruzzi, at least for the design and planning, was built starting from 1519 but the stone cutters were still working on the windows in 1612. The front, without arcades, stands on an escarp basement, the «piano nobile» is marked by a cornice with methopes and triglyphs. In order to recall the Roman public baths, which were probably located in an area near the palace, the Albergati family had a few ancient inscriptions walled in the arcaded courtyard (n. 26).

1. Basilica di S. Paolo Maggiore (17th century). 2. Collegio di Spagna: the court with two rows of arches and the little steeple of the church S. Clemente. 3. Church S. Clemente: inside.

From 1861 to 1865, via Saragozza was enlarged and its layout modified; the Porta with three arches and with crenellated side keeps was finished by Enrico Brunetti Rodati in 1859 as an enlargement for the Medieval gate.

Just outside of Porta Saragozza, in via Bellinzona 6, we come to the **Chiesa di San Giuseppe dei Cappuccini**, a building with measured Neoclassical features, remodelled in 1841-44 according to the design of Filippo Antolini over the area once occupied by a razed Romanesque-Gothic church: the old place of worship, built by a master called Rolando in 1273 for the jurist Egidio Foscarari, had taken the denomination of St. Mary Magdalene of Valle di Pietra and had housed the Dominican nuns until 1566, year in which the Order of the Serviti took it over by changing its name into St. Joseph's; it passed to the Capuchins in 1818.

The paintings and reliefs in this church form an interesting display of the 19th-century artistic production in Bologna and Emilia.

The following works are especially interesting: in the first chapel on the right, the large polychromatic terracotta group of *Pietà and St. Francis of Assisi* by Angelo Piò (1727); in the third ne on the right the *Holy Family*, called the Madonna of Mercy, a detached fresco attributed by the tradition to Annibale Carracci; on the high-altar, the *Wedding of the Virgin* by Adeodato Malatesta. From the elegant cloister built by Giovanni Antonio Conti (1718-22), in which an important 13th-century high-relief with the *Saints Peter and Paul* attributed to the «Master of the Deacon of St. Stephen's» can be seen, we reach the **Museo di San Giuseppe**. It is a large collection of works from Capuchins' churches and monasteries of the Romagna Province, which was started in 1923 by father Leonardo Montalti from Mercato Saraceno (1891-1942), and arranged by him from 1928 onward with the help of father Umile Negri from Camugnano (1892-1956). It was later rearranged and housed in a more functional place by father Celso Mazani (1923-1982) in 1970-73; the layout of the museum was designed by Leone Pancaldi. *Visits are possible on booking* (tel. n. 410545).

The Museum comprises 93 paintings, such as: the *Enthroned Virgin* by Pietro Lianori (15th century); a *Crucifix* on panel by Marco Zoppo (15th century); from the 16th century: *Virgin with Child* by Innocenzo da Imola; *Crucifixion and Saints* by Prospero Fontana; *Stigmata of St. Francis* by Denjs Calvaert; *Crucifixion and Saints* by Bartolomeo Passarotti. From the 17th century: *Death of St. Francis* by Leonardino; *St. Francis* by Bartolomeo Cesi. From the 18th century: *Glory of St. John the Nepomucene* by Giuseppe M. and Luigi Crespi; *St. Peter* and *St. Paul* by Giuseppe M. Crespi; *St. Gaetano*, the *Holy Family*, and the *Deposition* by the Gandolfi painters. The 19th century is also quite well represented. Among the sculptures: the *Madonna Sedes Sapientiae*, a terracotta group by Zaccaria Zacchi from Volterra (16th century); a terracotta *Pietà* by Camillo Mazza (17th century), *St. Giuseppe Benedetto Labre*, a wax work attributed to Angelo Piò; *Christ's Burial* with small marble figures from the 14th century; *Magdalene*, a polychromatic terracotta work by Sebastiano Sarti, also called Rodelone (18th century).

MUSEO STORICO DIDATTICO DELLA TAPPEZZERIA

Villa Spada, via di Casaglia 1-3, at the corner of via Saragozza, is a luxurious neoclassical vacation residence which the Marquis Giacomo Zambeccari commissioned from the Lugano architect Giovanni Martinetti (Bironico 1753-Bologna 1830) around 1790. Completed in 1749, the «Ravone Palace» - named after the nearby stream - was connected by the Marquis himself to his lovely park at the foot of the hills by a small terraced Italian garde, created with the contribution of the sculptor Giacomo De Maria, who embellished it with statues (the only survivor, an imposing Hercules of «slag»). In 1820 the complex changed ownership to the Roman prince Clemente Spada Veralli, who in order to expand it purchased the adjoining property of S. Alò in 1829, where he had a neo-Medieval tower built by the architect Marco Malvezzi, who also renovated the palace, which since then has been called Villa Spada. Here the Barnabite father Ugo Bassi, chaplain of the Garibaldi legions evacuated from Rome, was imprisoned and condemned to death at the beginning of August in 1849.

---

1. Porta Saragozza, 14th century, enlarged 1859. 2. Arco Bonaccorsi (17th century): here begins the Portico of S. Luca. 3. Church S. Giuseppe dei Cappuccini (19th century). 4. Meloncello Arch, by Dotti (18th century). 5. Villa Spada, by Martinetti (18th century): Seat of the Tapestry Museum.

Villa Spada, recovered and restored after long abandonment, since 1990 has been the site of the Historical-Didactic Drapery Museum, founded in 1966 by the passion of the Bolognese draper Vittorio Zironi, and which was operated for a quarter of a century (1966-1990) in the Salina Brazzetti bulding in via Barberia. The collection of over 6000 pieces is intended to reveal the history of fabrics and the various processing and restoration techniques. The ancient tradition of hand-made and hand-embroidered fabrics is documented along with the fluorishing legion of craftsmen who practiced this trade. The items shown here are brocades, damask fabric, flag cloth, velvet, Jacquard and Gobelin weaving patterns, block-printed Indian cloth and hundreds of many other types of precious and artistic textiles; also old hand-looms (one for braids from the 14th century, and an 18th-century wooden loom converted in the 19th century with the Jacquard system), tools for upholstery and related objects (such as studs and tacks, trimmings, frames, blocks, borders, fringes, fittings, bands, etc.): an extraordinary display of materials ranging throughout Europe, Africa and Asia for time span ranging from the Early-Middle Ages to the Liberty style. Among the most valuable items, let us mention the following: 18th cent. silk wedding sonnets; a broccatello cloth which covered the Christian images in the St. Sophia's Mosque in Instanbul; *lampasso* from the 8th century originally on the «golden altar» of S. Ambrogio church in Milan; the moiré *canopy of the Madonna di S. Luca* from 1870; 50 *banners* of the Arts' Guilds, donated by the Municipality.

Among the display rooms, the Gallery is magnificent with its reliefs by De Maria, the *Boschereccia* room, painted by a follower of Martinelli; the *Sundial Room*, vast and decorated by the lovely Zephyr modelled by De Maria, used for conventions.

The Drapery Museum (425030), directed by the architect Stefano Zironi, is open to visitors daily from 9 a.m. to 1 p.m. Closed Mondays and holidays.

Villa delle Rose, a late 18th-century buildin₂ with arcade and an encompassing open gallery stands nearby (via Saragozza, 232) at the end o an evocative stairway. It was raised for the Cel la family over a hillock, called Monte Franco on the place where the Spannocchi country palac had once stood. The Italian garden, with preciou aromatic plants, and also some exotic ones, i really interesting. The palace, which passed late into the hands of the Armandi Avogli family, be come Municipal property, destined to be used a a public park and for cultural activities, in 191 after the specific bequest of Nerina de Piccoli the widow of Count Guelfo. Guido Zucchin placed there the **Municipal Modern Art Gallery** rearranged by Francesco Arcangeli (1961) afte the devastation brought by the war, and move in 1975 in piazza della Costituzione (see pag 213). Villa delle Rose is still a section of th Gallery and is to be used as an art gallery for tem porary exhibitions or as a meeting hall for artis tic and cultural events. Near the villa there ar sculptures in bronze and marble dating back t 19th and 20th centuries. The two *Sleepin₂ Venuses* by Cincinnato Baruzzi are quite out standing, as the *bronze reliefs with fauns* by Si verio Monteguti, the big *nude figures* in bronz and the marble *Twilight* by Giuseppe Romagno li, and the *Cassandra* by Ercole Drei.

1. Tapestry Museum: an exhibition hall. 2. Tapestry Mus um: loom for trimmings (14th century). 3. Basilica of th Madonna di S. Luca, by Dotti. 4. The internal brightness c the sactuary. 5. Partial view of the portico rising to the hil.

192

4

ASILICA SANTUARIO ELLA MADONNA DI S. LUCA

The historical origins of this big shrine located on the Guardia hill date back to 1192, when ngelica di Caicle, who wanted to lead a religious fe, donated to the Canons of St. Mary of Reno me plots on the hill on which they were to help er on building a monastery.

As a consequence, the bishop of Bologna, Gerdo di Ghisla, laid on 25th May 1194 the foundtion stone of a small church, which was dedited to St. Mary of the Guardia Hill and in hich a beautiful image of the Virgin with Child, ill venerated today, was placed.

In 1433, Graziolo Accarisi, a jurist and a member of the Council of the Elders, suggested to move solemnly the image of Mary from the hill and to parade it through the town in public processions as a way to ask God for the end of the heavy rains which were ruining the crops: when the holy image passed through the arch of porta Saragozza, the rains stopped. This event further increased the devotion of the people, leading the bishop of Bologna, the blessed Nicolò Albergati, and the Municipal Council to repeat the transfer of the sacred image from the hill to the town every year with a public procession, as is still done today. The enlargement and remodelling of the small church on the hill, works which were completed in 1481, year of the shrine's consecration, had also become necessary.

In 1459, Accarisi also published a spurious ac-

193

count which, in consideration of the fact that the most ancient images of the Madonna were usually called «of St. Luke» by the people, attributed the painting kept on the Guardia hill to the Evangelist and said it had been brought to Bologna from Constantinopolis by a pilgrim.

In 1674, in order to ease the ascent and descent of the yearly processions carrying the image, and by the intervention of the priest Don Lodovico Generoli, who organized an impressing fund-raising campaign, in which all the citizens of Bologna and the countryside participated, the building of the famous arcade, the longest in the world, was started. With its 666 arches, this arcade winds up the hill for 3.796 km. climbing up a slope of about 200 metres and links the shrine to the town's gate.

It was planned in simple but very sturdy features by Architect Gian Giacomo Monti (1620-1692) and was completed in 1732 with the raising of the monumental **Arch of Meloncello** which joins the flat section of the arcade with the one climbing up the hill at about the three-hundredth arch of the arcade. It was planned by Architect Carlo Francesco Dotti (1678-1759).

The start of the new shrine's building was announced by the peal of all the church bells ringing throughout the town on 26th July 1723. Of the previous small church, only the main chapel, already remodelled according to a Baroque taste between 1706 and 1713, was left untouched.

The planner and works' supervisor was Architect Dotti who designed the shrine as a a gi-

ant reliquary, left standing by itself on the hill top, among the greenery. The unmistakable out line of the hill crowned by the shrine, visible from the whole surrounding plain, has become a pre cise reference point for the traveller coming to Bologna and a symbol of home and affection for its people.

Two marble statues by Bernardino Comett (1716), portraying the Saints Luke and Mark stand at the sides of the Shrine's entrance.

Inside we can admire: on the second altar to the left, a quite remarkable giant canvas by Donato Creti (1671-1749) representing the *Vir gin with Child in Glory with the Patron Saint of Bologna* and, in the main chapel, the marble altar designed by Architect Angelo Venturoli in 1815, which stands out in the middle of an area decorated in the 18th century with marble bronzes and encompassing scenes frescoed in the vaults by Vittorio Bigari (1692-1776).

The invaluable ancient image of the *Virgin with Child*, which has attracted throngs of pil grims and worshippers since the 12th century, i kept in the niche, high above, made prominen by the vast Baroque decorations surrounding it

The image, painted on a wooden panel and or nated with embossed reliefs, belongs to the type of Byzantine iconography called Madonna «Hodigitria» (that is bearer, carrying the Child in her arms), which, according to a Christian tra dition dating back to the 6th century, had origi nated from an image painted by the Evangelis Luke. The Shrine's image, instead, was made in Italy in the late 12th century, according to the style of the so-called «Crusader's icones», tha is the paintings which had derived from the close contact with the Eastern art of the Holy Land during the Crusades.

After the very elaborate screen made in 1767 by Pietro Fontana according to the design o Pietro Loraschi, we come to, on the first altar to the left, a *Virgin with Child, St. Dominic and the Mysteries of the Rosary*, an early painting by Guido Reni (1575-1642), who was so profound ly devoted to the Madonna of St. Luke that he climbed the hill on foot every week as a sign o his devotion.

In the next altar there is a large canvas by
[D]onato Creti with the *Crowning of the Virgin*
[am]ong hosts of angels and saints, and in the small
[ch]apel to the left of that same altar, a beautiful
[De]position, a polychromatic terracotta work at-
[tri]butable to Gaetano Gandolfi (late 18th cen-
[tu]ry).
In the dome, the *Madonna of Peace* was fres-
[co]ed by Giuseppe Cassioli in 1922-1932.

[L]A CERTOSA

[C]hiesa di S.Girolamo della Certosa (via Cer-
[to]sa, 18). The famous jurist Giovanni d'Andrea
[ca]lled the «Arcidottore», friend of Cino da
[Pi]stoia and Petrarca, called the Carthusian
[m]onks to Bologna in 1333 and provided them
[wi]th landplots in the town's outskirts in which
[to] build their monastery whose foundation stone
[wa]s laid on 17th April of the following year. The
[wo]rks, however, took impetus only after 1339,
[wh]en the Carthusian architect brother Galgano
[di] Vanni Baroccio was sent to Bologna from the
[M]aggiano monastery near Siena.
[B]eside supervising the building of the older
[clo]isters, he carried out the works in church as
[we]ll giving it the features which are still visible
[tod]ay: a single nave and peculiar inverse T plan.
[Th]e church was consecrated on 2nd July 1359.

Only in 1588 was the huge Chapel cloister, into
which the cloistered monks' cells had once
looked, added behind the apse. In the beginning
of the 17th century Architect Tommaso Martelli
raised, beside the 14th century small belfry, the
imposing bell-tower, one of the sturdier and more
harmonious steeple in town.

3

The church's inside is still separated by a strong screen: in the first section, once set for the faithful, there are two side chapels, one dedicated to *St. Jerome* (the altar-piece with the *Saint's Communion* is a copy by Clemente Alberti of the original painting by Agostino Carracci), the other to *St. Bruno*, the founder of the Carthusian Order (the altar-piece is by Bartolomeo Cesi); in the second section, once for the monks, there is the magnificent *wooden choir*, splendidly and elegantly carved and inlaid. The stalls near the entrance were made by Biagio de' Marchi in 1539 while the last six stalls in each side were later added by Giovanni Battista Natali and Antonio Levante in 1611; the dais and the music-stand, also by de' Marchi, are quite outstanding.

The paintings in the Main Chapel, representing the *Prayer of Jesus in the Garden of Getsemani*, the *Crucifixion* and the *Deposition* are by Bartolomeo Cesi (1616).

The large canvasses decorating the upper section of the nave were made by several painters around the mid-17th century. By starting from the entrance and walking along the left-hand side, they represent respectively: the *Baptism of Christ* (by Elisabetta Sirani); the *Supper at the Pharisee's House* (by Giovanni Andrea Sirani); the *Miraculous Draught of St. Peter* (by Francesco Gessi); the *Risen Christ Appearing to the Virgin* (by Lorenzo Pasinelli); the *Triumphal Entry of Jesus in Jerusalem* (by Pasinelli); *Jesus Chasing the Merchants from the Temple* (by Ges-

si); the *Judgement's Day* (by Domenico Canti), and the *Ascension* (by Giovanni Maria Ga from Bibiena).

On the right side of the church we can find the small but evocative *cloister of the Madonna* where several images of Mary previously belong ing to churches destroyed or deconsecrated 1797 during the Napoleonic period had bee placed. During that same year, the Carthusia Order was also suppressed and the Monastery b came in 1801 a Municipal cemetery, as is still to day. It has, therefore, been embellished and dec rated by innumerable artworks, especially statu and monuments, mostly during the 19th and 20 centuries.

Here famous personalities have been burie such as the politician Marco Minghetti, th painters Gaetano and Giorgio Morandi (his bu is by Giacomo Manzù), the musician and con poser Ottorino Respighi, the writer Riccardo Ba chelli, and many University teachers and le turers: the best-known among them is certain the poet Giosuè Carducci.

In 1827 the small, quaint *Evangelical Cemeter* was added to the Catholic necropolis, with Doric portico on three sides; in the same year the nearby field of the Israeli Cemetery was als opened.

1. Small cloister of the Madonnas (15th century). 2. Via G liera: Bonasoni Palace.

XTH ITINERARY

Basilica of S. Maria Maggiore
Church of S. Giorgio in Poggiale
Church of the Saints Gregorio and Siro
Cathedral of S. Pietro
Civic Medieval and Renaissance Museum - Ghisilardi-Fava Palace
Montagnola Gardens
Municipal Modern Art Gallery
Aldini-Valeriani Technical Institute - Museum and Laboratory of Machinery-School-Industry

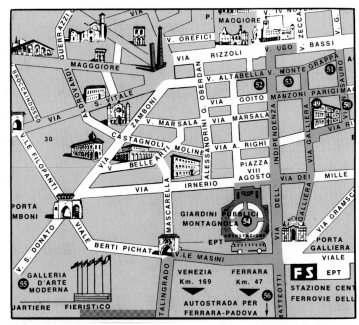

Via Galliera

Via Galliera corresponded, according to the experts, to the *cardo* maximus of the Roman towns, that is the road running in a north to south direction and crossing the *decumanus* maximus running from east to west (today's via U. Bassi and via Rizzoli), as was common to all Roman towns and their division into centuries. In the palaces of via Galliera, which is somewhat less congested than other nearby traffic arteries and with less public buildings, one can still read the history of many senatorial families in Bologna. Therefore, the aristocratic and rich features of this street appear evident.

Palazzo Torfanini (n. 4) still retains an arcade probably dating back to the mid-16th century, while the upper section of the building dates from the 18th century. In fact, the Duke of Modena bought the palace and had it remodelled by Alfonso Torreggiani (1732). The architect carried out its work quite carefully, maintaining some of the former features, such as the artistic capitals (1544); he also planned for the «piano nobile» a series of windows with elegant cornices which mark the front with discretion and sobriety without sharp contrast between the time-differing elements.

Palazzo dal Monte (ns. 3-5), attributed to Forigine, dates back to the 16th century and, in spite of the presence of arcades in its front, maintains its proper characteristics which make it stand out in the street, such as its stylobates and the correct application of Classical architectural orders as, for example, in the piers supporting five arches, embellished by Corinthian half-columns.

The jutting skirt roofing and the moulding of the «piano nobile» windows, spaced by Corinthian columns, set the harmonious passage between empty and full spaces, in perfect symmetry with the underlying arcade. The inside 18th century decoration is characterized in the trompe-l'oeil perspective in the staircase hall by a fresco of Gaetano Gandolfi representing the *Rape of*

197

Deianeira. In the rooms there are paintings by Serafino Barozzi representing the allegories of the *Four Seasons* and the *Nine Muses*, among other subjects.

Casa dalle Tuate (n. 6) retains quite visible two portraits: one is the profile of Giovanni II Bentivoglio placed on the pilasters at the corner with via San Giorgio, the other on top of a capital in the arcade belongs to an unknown person. The identification of Giovanni II is proved correct by an inscription carved on the marble, which says «DIV. IO. B. II. P. P.». According to a quali-

fied interpretation, the capital used in the Da Tuate palace came originally from Bentivogl palace, which had stood in the area now occupie by the Municipal Theatre.

Palazzo Aldrovandi, today's Montanari Pala (n. 8), is a majestic Baroque building started 1725 with a brickwork and Istrian stone façad erected according to the design of Alfonso To reggiani (1744-52). The architect placed in t front marvelous and imaginative iron grates order to «counterbalance» the insufficient heig of the ground floor section, built as such accord ing to the wish of the owner. The grand *stairca* by Angelini and the frescoes in the *Gallery* (to day's Municipal library) with the *Fasts of the A drovandi family* by Vittorio Bigari and Stefar Orlandi are quite outstanding.

Basilica of S. Maria Maggiore (at n. 10) is Romanesque church consecrated in 1187 an renewed by Paolo Canali in 1665. In it we ca admire a nice altar-piece by Orazio Samacchi (*Madonna with child and Saints*) and two pol chrome terracotta statues by Giovanni Zacc (16th century).

Thanks to the timely restoration carried out b the Committee for the Historical and Artist Protection of Bologna, we can now admire a fe late 15th-century homes which have bee

1. Tanari Palace. 2. Aldrovandi Montanari Palace, 18th ce tury. 3. Basilica S. Maria Maggiore (12th-17th century). Porta Galliera (17th century) and the remains or the ancie Fortress.

preserved: **Casa Cervi** (n. 13), **Casa Argelati** (n. 15) and **Palazzo Felicini** (n. 14).

The fact that the respect for the tradition was retained during the Renaissance period is further proven by the presence of arcades, in whose capitals the artists seem to have given full rein to their imagination. Quite invaluable 15th-century terracotta works can be admired in **Casa de' Buoi** (n. 35), where rows of dragons decorate the arcade's borders and a group of cupids lie placidly among intertwining vine leaves in the skirt roofing: the production of these decorative terracottas was not only for the local market, but it was also destined to be exported.

Underneath the arcade of **Palazzo Tanari** (n. 8) there is a carved group of statues from the end of the 18th century by Giacomo De Maria: it represents a *Holy Family* lovingly offered to the passer-by's devotion. Christina of Sweden, the Queen that, after converting to Catholicism, chose to live in Italy among writers and artists, slept once during a visit to the town in Palazzo Tanari, which is embellished by the paintings of Cancelli, Pedrini and Martinelli.

Palazzo Bonasoni (n. 21) retains an arcade with seven spans supported by columns with mid-shaft annulets: the Composite capitals repeat in their 16th-century motifs an imaginative and wild iconography of dolphins, palms, festoons and putti. A similarly rich decoration is found in the windows' cyma, which seem here to imitate the foldings of draperies.

Palazzo Merendoni (n. 26), rebuilt by Raimondo Compagnini (1775) retains an important staircase enriched by sculptures and stucco works of Domenico Piò and by a fresco by Gaetano Gandolfi.

Palazzo Savioli (n. 40), which was also started by Compagnini, belonged to the poet and historian from Bologna Ludovico Savioli (1729-1804), the author of a small canzoniere titled «Loves» and of the «Bologna's Annals».

The layout of via Galliera, once the meeting centre of the «social» life, ends with the **Porta**, built in 1661 by Bartolomeo Provaglia in place of the almost completely dilapidated 13th- century gate. This gate, with its severe and imposing features, mirrors certain trends in the Baroque art specific of this area: the smooth ashlar facing of the basement, developing along an horizontal plane, is counteracted by the marked verticality of the coupled lesenes, the half-columns and the superimposed central body.

We can observe on the left of the gate the old remains of the Galliera castle, authentic relics from the past. The castle was built for the representatives of the Pope in order to better control the town under a military viewpoint: rebuilt five times, the fortress was razed as many times by the people of Bologna during riots and revolts. The last destruction dates back to 1511, during the Papacy of Julius II. Historians recalled that the stronghold was enclosed by ramparts, twelve-ells wide, and provided with eight bartizans.

The deconsecrated church of **San Giorgio in Poggiale** stands in via Nazario Sauro 20. Already documented at least since the 13th century, but possibly of Lombard origins, it was called «in Poggiale» from the small hillock, now disappeared, on which it stood. It was rebuilt from 1589 to 1633 on late-Renaissance style according to the design by Tommaso Martelli; the beautiful Serliana window in the façade is one of its more remarkable features. Destroyed by bomb-

ings on 25th September 1943, it was left in ruins. Bought by the Cassa di Risparmio (Savings' Bank) of Bologna, it was restored in the years 1974-1978, and now important art shows at national and international levels, concerts, symposia and conferences are held there. The former church houses also the invaluable *Collezioni d'arte e di storia* (Art and History Collections) of the Cassa di Risparmio: a rich collection acquired in many years, which is kept here not only as an exhibition but also for studies and conservation. The collections are divided up into several important sections. *Numismatic section*, with more than 2,500 medals and 1,600 coins from the Mint of Bologna (1191-1861) and Antignate, 150 small plaques, badges, cards, weights and measures. *Paintings' section* with about 400 pieces of extremely high quality (such as: the *Annunciation* by Francesco Francia; *Virgin with Child and Saints* by Biagio Pupini; the *Knights' Contest* by Giovannino da Capugnano from the 16th century; *Death of the Blessed Bernardo Tolomei* by Domenico M. Canuti; a *Battle Scene* and two *Still Lifes from a Hunt* by Giuseppe M. Crespi; *Moses Saved from the Waters* by Donato Creti; *Blind Beggar* by Gaetano Gandolfi; *Portrait of a Painter* by Telemaco Signorini; a *Wood* by Luigi Bertelli; *Self-portrait* by Flavio Bertelli. *Drawings' section*, with about 2,200 pieces from the 16th century onwards, with designs by Carracci family, Rainaldi, Mitelli, Creti, Crespi, Gandolfi, Bigari, Panfili, Jarmorini, Giani, Calvi, Basoli, Serra, Fantuzzi, Savini and many others. *Etchings' section* with more than 7,200 pieces, including works by Blaeu, Mattioli, Mitelli, Francesco M. Francia, Panfili, Raimondi, Canuti, Serra, Romagnoli, Morandi and others. *Photographic*

section, with about 20,000 plates originally from several collections (Romagnoli, Poppi, Zagnoli Piazzi, Fantini). The collections also includ more than 200 water-colours, 425 old and modern lithographs, 20 ceramic objects, 17,00 manuscripts and publications, thousands of post cards.

For a visit to the Collections of the Cassa di Rispar mio (entrance from via Morgagni, parallel to via N Sauro), please call the Collections' office, tel. n 230727.

Chiesa dei Santi Gregorio e Siro (via Mont Grappa, 13). The building of this church wa started on 5th March 1532 by the master builder Tibaldo Tibaldi and Giovanni Antonio d Milano according to the design of Architect An drea da Valle from Istria for the Venetian Con gregation of St. George in Alga; it was consecrat ed in 1579.

With its quite large single nave flanked by tw rows of chapels, all of the same size, this churc is a typical example of Counter-Reformation ar chitecture because it allows worshipers to see th high-altar from every angle and, therefore, fo low the service held there.

In 1676, the canons were replaced by the Regu lar Clergy of the Ministers of the Sick, the orde founded by St. Camillo de' Lellis and therefor called «Camilliani». After the church had bee heavily damaged by an earthquake, they commis

1. S. Giorgio in Poggiale: the façade (16th-17th centuries
2. Church of SS. Gregorio e Siro: the Façade (1870). 3. V dell'Indipendenza from the south.

ioned the reconstruction of the façade and the ault, according to the design of Angelo Venturoi, in 1780.

The coat of arms which decorates the façade elongs to the Ghisilieri noble family that lived ere till 1445. The bell-tower is a 16th- century emodelling of the much older tower of that ristocratic family (14th century).

Among the many invaluable paintings decorating the church's altars let us recall at least the following: the epic canvas by Ludovico Carracci 1555-1619) narrating the double triumph of *St. George* over the dragon on Earth, and of the *Archangel Michael* over the demons in Heaven; the magnificent *Baptism of Christ*, a pellucid masterpiece of Annibale Carracci (1585), then only wentyfive years old; *St. Gregorius Magnus Conerting a Heretic* by Denjs Calvaert on the highltar (1581); the *Assumption of the Virgin* by Camillo Procaccini (1582); the *Saints Andrew, Lorenzo Giustiniani and Anthony Abbot at the Feet of the Virgin*, a severely spiritual work by Lucio Massari (1569-1632); and finally the airy *Glory of St. Camillo de' Lellis* painted by Giovan Battista Pittoni from Veneto in 1746.

The decoration on the altar frontals of the side hapels is also quite interesting as the frame in the main chapel, all of them, sandstone works inely carved and partially painted and gilded, attributable to Andrea da Formigine and dating back to the mid- 16th century.

Marcello Malpighi, the famous anatomist and ride of the 17th- century medical school in Bologna, was buried here in 1694.

In via Nazario Sauro, the fourth side street at the right of via Ugo Bassi, stands **Palazzo Lambertini** (n. 18), today's the seat of the Liceo Classico M. Minghetti, a building dating from the second half of the 16th century. Up to 1871, the members of the Felsinea Freemasons' lodge (one of them was the poet Giosuè Carducci) held their meetings here. If we continue along via N. Sauro and, at the crossing with via Riva di Reno, we turn right, we reach: **Palazzo Gnudi** (n. 77), planned by Francesco Tadolini (1796), which still retains an 18th-century staircase, a magnificent hall with stucco decorations in Empire style and a room in which Gaetano Gandolfi represented the *Sacrifice of Iphigeneia*.

Via dell'Indipendenza

The layout of via dell'Indipendenza was planned in 1857 in order to set up a communication artery linking the town's centre to the RAILWAY STATION, whose building was planned or the following year. Starting from the second alf of the 19th century, after a series of works arried out between 1885 and 1888, via dell'Indipendenza became the central traffic pole for the own, soon replacing the parallel via Galliera, which up to then had been the town's fashionable street.

Via dell'Indipendenza starts in front of piaza del Nettuno and at the corner with today's via Rizzoli. In the street's first section, once called he «flower corner», the 16th-century **Case Scapi** are now standing. One of them (n. 3) includes Medieval tower with a nice offset window, crowned by double arches.

Palazzina Majani (n. 4) offers, despite modern additions, an example of Art Nouveau architecture, a work by A. Sezanne (1908).

3

CATTEDRALE DI S. PIETRO

It seems that before the 8th century the town did not have a cathedral and that the bishop resided in different parishes without a permanent see. Only between the 8th and the 9th centuries was a permanent Bishop's palace probably built on this area, connected to a church dedicated to St. Peter, which was completely gutted by a ravaging fire in August 1131.

After several years, the bishop Giovanni V had the church rebuilt in Romanesque-Gothic style. On 8th July 1184 Pope Lucius III consecrated the church which retained the old dedication to St. Peter, the saint that was considered at that time the town's first patron saint and protector and whose image was minted on some of the oldest Bologna's coins.

Here, the University of Bologna celebrated its solemn ceremonies, such as the awarding of degrees, which was the prerogative of the Cathedral's Archdeacon.

Between 1575 and 1597, the archbishop, Cardinal Gabriele Paleotti, had the main chapel completely rebuilt according to the design of Architect Domenico Tibaldi. In fact, the chapel was near collapsing and the next bishop, Alfonso Paleotti, after long wavering, commissioned the complete reconstruction in larger scale of the church's nave and aisles to the Barnabite architect Ambrogio Mazenta from Milan in 1605.

In 1610, the new archbishop, Cardinal Scipione Borghese, nephew of Pope Paul V, called from Rome the architects Carlo Maderno and Flaminio Ponzio, who drew a new project, soon opposed by the local architect Floriano Ambrosini, who was supervising the works.

Among rivalries and uncertainties, the architect Nicolò Donati was called in as mediator. He opened up in all its height the dome over the main chapel towards the nave, which had been built by Tibaldi, and raised the giant vault (60-metres large), the largest in Europe at that time. The building was continued by Lodovico Amatori for the church's inside according to a design by the Architect Giovan Battista Natali. The church remained without façade for over a century and only between 1743 and 1755 was it completed by adding two chapels, one at each side, and the front, thanks to the archbishop Cardinal Prospero Lambertini, later Pope Benedict XIV, who had commissioned it to Architect Alfonso Torreggiani.

1. Cathedral of S. Pietro: the façade (18th century). 2. The massive Romanesque belfry (13th century). 3. The vast Baroque inside. 4. Prone lion, a 13th-century marble work.

The powerful bell-tower, built by master Alberto (who had also built the Arengo tower) in the second half of the 13th century by including and raising by three tiers the round belfry of the older Cathedral (9th cent), is particularly remarkable. In the 18th century, thanks to the building's extraordinary solidity, given by its two concentric bell-towers, bells were started to be rung in the «fashion of Bologna», that is by making them turn rythmically around their pivot by 360° with the help of strong ropes.

The cathedral's inside is amazingly vast. The two *holy-water stoups* near the door are supported by two lions in red Verona marble, which gave their name to the famous side door built by master Ventura between 1220 and 1223 for the Romanesque-Gothic basilica.

Other remains of that door are placed in the first chapel to the left together with a large *baptismal font* made by Ferdinando Saint Urbain from Lorraine (18th century).

In the third chapel, decorated for the archbishop, Cardinal Lambertini, before he was elected Pope, we can admire the nice painting by Donato Creti (1671-1749) representing *St. Ignatius in front of the Virgin with Child in Glory*.

The main chapel (by Architect Domenico Tebaldi, 1575) presents: in the vault the *Eternal Father in Glory and Angels*, a fresco by Prospero Fontana (1584) completed by Alessandro Tiarini (1616) in the arch towards the nave; in the big

4

lunette, the *Annunciation*, the last work by Ludovico Carracci (1618-19); in the apse's vault, the fresco representing *St. Peter Receiving the Keys from Christ* is by Giovan Battista Fiorini (design and execution of the Glory in the upper part) and by Cesare Aretusi (the figures), who completed it in 1595.

In the vast crypt we can see: a precious and refined wood *Crucifixion* from the 12th century, originally from the older cathedral the remains of which can be seen in the *archeological area* beneath the current church, which can be entered directly from the crypt.

Back in the church (the stoup near the side door was originally a part of the old Lions' door),

by walking down the right aisle we come to: on the first altar, *St. Charles Tending the Poor* by Creti; on the second one (by Architect Camillo Rusconi, first half of the 18th century), the altar-piece and the other canvasses are by Marco Antonio Franceschini (1648-1729), the fresco on the cupola (*St. Peter Inspires Pope Celestinus to Name St. Petronius as the Bishop of Bologna*) is the last work by Vittorio Bigari (1776); on the third altar (by Architect Angelo Venturoli, 1789) *St. Peter Consecrating St. Apollinare's Church* is by Ercole Graziani (1688-1765).

The fourth chapel is also quite outstanding: the relic of St. Ann, donated in 1433 by Henry VI, King of England, to the blessed Nicolò Albergati, bishop of Bologna, is kept there inside an enamelled 15th-century glass case framed by a nice marble perspective made in 1906 according to a design by Edoardo Collamarini.

In the last chapel was inserted in June 1992 the enormous group of the *Pietà*, made in terracotta by Alfonso Lombardi (1497-1537), taken from the crypt, where it has been since 1584 by the will of Cardinal Paleotti.

---

1. Frescoes by Prospero Fontana in the chancel's vault. 2. 12th-century Crucifix in wood. 3. Via del Monte: Boncompagni Palace (16th century). 4. Via Manzoni: courtyard o, Ghisilardi Fava Palace (15th century).

Via Altabella starts on the right side of the Cathedral of St. Peter. The **Bishop's Palace**, from the 13th century, as we can see in the high external arcade, is located in this street. In the inner courtyard we can see the hand of Architect Domenico Tibaldi in this example of Counter-Reformation architecture, made in the last decades of the 16th century according to the strict religious norms of that time.

By walking down via S. Alò to the right, we come to the **Prendiparte Tower**, also known as the *Coronata* (Crowned) for the drawing in its offset.

In via del Monte (2nd side street to the right of via dell'Indipendenza) we can see **Palazzo Boncompagni** (n. 8), completed in 1545 and by tradition attributed to Vignola.

Its escarp base and horizontal spacing elements are interrupted by the magnificent portal, linking the basement to the first floor, marked by windows framed by double spiral mouldings. The perspective effect of the entrance hall is evocatively produced by the elegant door combined with the spiral staircase.

MUSEO CIVICO MEDIEVALE E DEL RINASCIMENTO

The Museo Civico Medievale e del Rinascimento (Civic Museum of Medieval and Renaissance Art) is located in **Palazzo Ghisilardi-Fava**, via Manzoni 4.

Opened in spring of 1985, this museum is located in a nice palace built between 1483 and 1491 according to a plan by master Zilio (Egidio) Montanari for the grand notary and chancellor of the Sixteen, Bartolomeo Ghisilardi. Bought by the

Counts Fava in 1810 and later passed to the Municipality, this building has been brought, through extensive restoration works carried out for over a decade with the most sophisticated and scientific criteria, to its pristine condition, by eliminating all the foreign elements that had been added in various times. The original structure has been strengthened and brought to light (for which, together with Palazzo Sanuti Bevilacqua, see pag. 168, it is considered the most complete and magnificent example of civilian architecture of 15th-century Bologna) and, through the restoration, the finding and identification of important older buildings have been made possible. Among these older structures, let us recall: the *Conoscenti tower* from the 13th century, and the remains (selenite ashlar wall section, coupled arches formed by blocks in the same material) of the *Palatium*, seat of the political and military powers in the town, located on the northwestern side of the *selenite town's walls* from the mid-7th century (large sections of which have now been shown) and demolished in 1115. The collections, which from 1881 to 1962 formed the Medieval section of the Museo Civico (today's formed only by the extremely important archeological section and therefore called Museo Civico Archeologico, see pag. 88) in the former Hospital of Death, were originally part of the Museum of Ferdinando Cospi (1605-1686), of the artworks arranged in Palazzo Poggi by Marsigli in 1709-12, and also included the floor grave-

4

stones and tombs belonging to suppressed churches, assembled together from 1866 onwards by Luigi Frati. Other older pieces, collected by Aldrovandi, or other ones from the 19th century by Palagi have come to this museum. Its aim is to illustrate the development of Medieval and early Renaissance art in Bologna, with many examples of Baroque and Mannerist art as well, in a logical and exhaustive approach including the links between the town and the Studium and the artistic circles and workshops in Italy and abroad. The so-called «minor arts» are particularly well attended to (ivory pieces, ceramics, glass objects, medals and coins, musical instruments, textiles, weapons, etc.) in a thorough exhibit ranging from the period in which Bologna was a Free-town to the one in which it was ruled by the Bentivoglio family, together with pieces from the «historical» collections. The future enlargement of the museum, by opening the connecting Palazzo Fava (16th century), entered from via Manzoni 2, has made it possible to place the collections of ceramics and musical instruments in five rooms with coffered ceilings and frescos (1584) by the Carraccis (lovely those with tales of Europe, the cycle of Tales from the Aeneid, and others with tales of Jason and the Golden Lamb).

All the items in the museum are accompanied by clear captions and explanations. The rational layout of the museum within a historical palace makes a visit to Palazzo Ghisilardi really worthwhile, and probably one of the most evocative in Italy.

Ground floor. Room 4, called of the Monu-

ments to the Studium's teachers: *Ark of Giovanni d'Andrea*, 1348, a marble work by Jacopo Lanfranchi from Venice; *Fragments of the ark o, Giovanni da Legnano*, 1383, by Pier Paolo Dalle Masegne; *Fragments of the ark of Carlo, Roberto and Riccardo da Saliceto*, 1403, by an unknown stone carver; *Ark of Bartolomeo de Saliceto*, 1411, a marble work by Andrea da Fiesole. In all the monuments for the University teachers found in this museum, and in all the floor gravestones, we should notice the extraordinary naturalism and extreme liveliness of expression of the carved images. In the center of the room are seven extraordinary limestone sculptures which still preserve remains of their original colouring. They may be dated to around 1390, and are from the niches in the façade of the Merchants' Building. Attributed to various artists, they were all influenced by the art of the Venetian Pier Paolo delle Masegne. They depict *Justice* (which could be by Pier Paolo himself) and, in bust form, six patron saints of Bologna: *Dominic, Peter, Florian, Ambrose, Petronius, Francis*). Room 5: jewellery a *lombard cross* in gold leaf from the 8th century. Room 6, monuments of various origins: a stone *cross* on a column, and a *cross with the*

1

agnus dei», also in stone, both from the 2th-13th centuries; *bronze hand-washing vessel from Lower Saxony*, 13th century; *Prayer in the Garden*, a carved ivory work of art from Northern Italy, 12th century. Room 7: *base of a stoup* with four male figures by a sculptor from the Po alley area, 13th century; *St. Ursula*, an embossed copper piece from the 14th century; a *statue of Pope Bonifatius VIII*, an exceptional piece in embossed copper over a wooden core by Manno Bandini from Siena, 1301; *Crucifixion*, European painted glass, 13th century; anthropomorphic bronze *candlestick* from Lower Saxony, 13th century; an extraordinary *cope of St. Dominic* (from St. Dominic's church), an English piece in linen and silk from the beginning of the 14th century, embroidered with 19 tales of the life of Christ and Mary and figures of angels and saints.

Basement. Room 8: *Gravestone of Filippino Desideri* by Arriguzzo Trevisano, 1315. Room 9: *statue of St. Peter Martyr*, a marble work by Giovanni di Balduccio; the *Peace stone* by the «master of Corrado Fogolini» from 1322, carved a celebration of the settling of a controversy risen between the students and the town. Room 10: *Tomb of Pietro Cerniti*, 1338, a stone work by Oso da Parma; the famous *Floor gravestone of Domenico Garganelli*, made around 1478 by Francesco del Cossa in limestone, variegated marble and bronze; the *Tomb of Bonifacio Galuzzi*, 1346, a variegated Istrian stone work by Jettino da Bologna; *Statue of the Virgin with Child*, called St. Mary of Bethlehem, a marble work from the 13th century. Room 11: *Tomb of Lorenzo Pini*, 1397, by Paolo di Bonaiuti. Room 2: powerful marble triptych (*Virgin with Child*, *Saints Peter and George*, *Angels* and a *Saint* in the only remining cusp) by Jacopo della Quercia and his workshop from the beginning of the 15th century; *Nativity scene*, a marble high-relief by Andrea da Fiesole. Room 13: *Floor gravestone of Bernardino Zambeccari*, a stone work by Andrea da Fiesole, 1424; *Tomb slab of Pietro Canonici*, a variegated stone work by Vincenzo Onofri, 1502; *Tomb of Matteo Gandoni*, 1330, from the workshop of Agostino di Giovanni and Angelo di Ventura.

First floor. Room 15: bronze statues and figures from the Renaissance to the Baroque period: *Model of the Neptune's statue* for the Fountain on the square, by Giambologna, 1564; the *Archangel Michael* by Alessandro Algardi; a *bust of Gregory XIII Boncompagni* by Alessandro Menganti, 1572; *bust of Gregory XV Ludovisi*, attributed to Gian Lorenzo Bernini, ca. 1621; among the bronze statuettes, *Marsyas* and the *Burial of Christ* by Andrea Briosco, known as Riccio; small *casket* with reliefs attributed to Severo di Ravenna (all works from the 16th century) and also sculptures by Vittoria, Aspetti, Giambologna, Campagna. Room 16: part of the collection of musical instruments from Europe

and other parts of the world, especially from the 16th and 17th centuries, is temporarily shown here as the permanent exhibition rooms, frescoed by the Carracci painters, in Palazzo Fava are being restored. The collection comprises many valuable pieces, such as: a *clavichord* by Vito de Transuntini, 1606; a *bass lute* by M. Stegher, 16th century; a *lute* by Magnus Tieffenbrucker junior, 1612; a *harpsychord* by Orazio Albana, 1628; a *larg mandolin* by Matteo Sellas, 1630; a *pochette* shaped as a dolphin by B. Bressano; a *psaltery* by Francesco Cessori, 18th century. Rooms 17 and 18: weapons, blades and fire-arms, mostly from the Crespi and Marsigli collections, including a *Blessed rapier* in steel and silver made in Rome in the 15th century for Ludovico Bentivoglio; a *plaque with St. George*, a painting by a follower of Francia, on a parchment stretched over a wood frame; a *composite armour for open battle* from Northern Italy, ca. 1570; a 15th- cen-

3

2

tury *horn* from the times of the Bentivoglio, a work from Emilia; a *cinquedea dagger*, etched with the Bentivoglio coat of arms, ca. 1500; a decorated and embossed *brocchiere* from the Milan school at the end of the 16th century; and also a stucco, *Veronica* by Francesco di Simone Ferrucci from Fiesole (15th century); a *glass tondo with a male head*, 15th century, attributed to Ercole Roberti; *stained-glass with Christ in Pietà* by an artist from Bologna, 15th century. Rooms 19 and 20 displaying Turkish weapons and others: a *pair of tschinken* (light archebus) with the Marsigli coat of arms from the 17th century (Silesia); *quivers* for arrows and bow, 17th century. Room 21, ivory and bone objects: a *box with the myth of Pyramos and Thysbe*, Embriachi workshop, 15th century; *triptych with the Vir-*

1

3

208

in and Child and *scenes of the life of Christ*, 14th-century French production; an African-Portuguese ivory *salt-box*, 15-16th centuries; *ba-in* with the stories of David, in ivory, deer an-ers and metal by J. M. Maucher from Germa-y (17th century). Room 22, glass: a *couple of ottles from Murano* from the 15th century with he Bentivoglio and Sforza coats of arms; a *blue oblet*, decorated and gilded from Murano, 15th entury; a *goblet* with small handles from Murano, 16th century; interlaced *display plate* rom Murano, 16th century; small *cup* in blown-lass and filigree from Murano, 18th century; a magnificent *perfume vial* made in Mesopothamia nd Assyria in the 13th century.

The collection of musical instruments and he rich *collection of Western ceramics* are be-ng prepared in the rooms of Palazzo Fava, where he Carraccis painted lovely frescos depicting mythological stories from Homer, Virgil, Flac-o. The collection of Western ceramics includes pproximately 300 pieces which illustrate the mazing development of this production from the 3th to the 19th centuries; it also exhibits pieces om many kilns and workshops, some more fa-ous than others but all very interesting (Faen-a, Ferrara, Imola, Bologna, Urbino, Pesaro, astel Durante — later Urbania —, Lodi, Vene-a, Albisola, Savona, Castelli, Cafaggiolo, Mon-lupo, Gubbio, etc.). Among the pieces from broad, let us recall the ones from Spain of Arab-inspiration (Manises) and Germany (Siegburg, öln, Frechen, Kreussen, Westerwald, etc.). We ould like to mention: the *ink-well with 4 Pa-on Saints of Bologna*, a majolica from Faen-a, 15th century; a *jug with a lady's bust* pierced y a dagger and the inscription «Love», a majol-

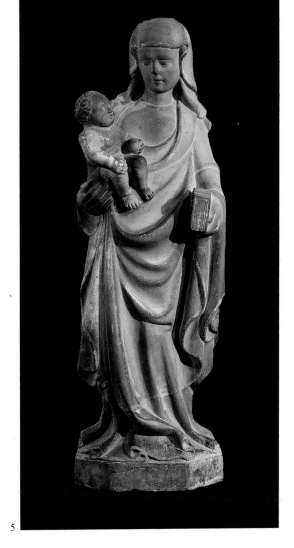

Giovanni di Balduccio: the martyr St. Peter (13th centu-. 2. The «Stone of Peace», 1322 (detail). 3. Francesco del ssa: floor tomb of Domenico Garganelli (ca. 1478). 4. Bet-o da Bologna: Sepulchre of Bonifacio Galluzzi (1346). 5. thlehem's Madonna, 13th century.

5

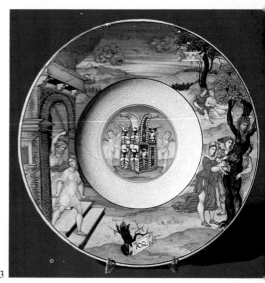

ica from Faenza, 1499; a *cup with Clement VII crowning Charles V*, a majolica of Casa Pirota, Faenza, ca. 1530; a *tagliere (plate) with the grief over a warrior-woman*, a majolica by Baldassarre Manara, Faenza ca. 1534; a *cup with Jesus in the house of Simon*, by Leonardo Solombrino, a majolica from Forlì from 1564; *albarello vase* with bearded old man, a majolica from Venice, ca. 1570; a *tagliere with the dream of Astiage*, a majolica by Francesco Xanto Avelli, Urbino 1536; *tagliere with Adonis and Mhyrra*, a majolica by Niccolò Pellipario from Urbino, 1525; *plate decorated with the Presentation of the Virgin*, 1532, majolica by Niccolò Pellipario polished in Gubbio by Giorgio Andreoli; a *trilobate basin with the triumph of Galathea* by Fontana from Urbino, ca. 1575; *Bacchus and Sylenus*, round earthenware from the Aldrovandi kilns in Bologna, end of the 18th century. The section on the grès from the Reno valley is also quite interesting (Colle Ameno of the Ghisilieri).

The *collection of codes and miniatures* comprises about 140 codes with matriculae, statutes and chorals, especially from the 13th to the 15th centuries in Bologna: the *matricula of the Drapers* is quite famous, a 1411 miniature from

Bologna, reproducing the lively activity of th «middle Market». The collection of *medals* really important; with its thousands of meda and coins, it illustrates the production of th Bologna's Mint along the centuries and it com prises really invaluable artistic and historica pieces. Among the Bentivoglio coins, let us reca the famous *testone* by the painter and goldsmit Francia and, among the medals, exceptiona pieces by Pisanello and Sperandio from the 15t century.

In February 1988 a new section (two room was opened; in it, the atmosphere of the Baroqu *rooms of wonders* has been created in order t stress the continuous interest for near and fa

1. Jean de Boulogne: sketch of the Neptune statue. 2. Jac po della Quercia: Triptych. 3. Niccolò Pellipario: plate wi Adonis and Mhyrra, ca. 1575. 4. Plate of St. George, scho of Francia. 5. Church of Madonna di Galliera: façade (151C

Visits on weekdays from 9 a.m. to 2 p.m.; on Sundays from 9 a.m.to 12,30 p.m.. The Museum is closed on Tuesday and on holidays falling within the week. Telephone n. 228912.

Chiesa di S. Maria di Galliera (via Manzoni, 3). This church was founded in 1304 and the image of the Virgin with Child, to which many miraculous events had been attributed, originally frescoed under the arcade adjacent to the church, was placed there in 1478.

Between 1479 and 1492 the church was completely rebuilt under the supervision of master Zilio (Egidio) di Battista Montanari with its beautiful flank decorated with terracotta works among which a *bust of the Saint*, attributed to Sperandio, can be seen inside a round cornice.

The façade was built in 1510 according to a design by Donato di Gajo da Cernobbio, but we do not know the name of the sculptor who skillfully carved the decorative elements, unfortunately now quite damaged.

In 1622, Pope Gregory XV (Alessandro Ludovisi from Bologna) gave this church to the brothers of the Oratory Congregation, founded by St. Filippo Neri. The congregation had the church enlarged and completely remodelled in the inside according to the design of Architect Giuseppe Torri in 1684.

The leaves of the main portal, carved in the 16th century, are quite interesting and the decorations in the vaults and in the apse, made by Giuseppe Marchesi, known as «Sansone» (1700-1771), are really refined. Marchesi also frescoed the vault of the first chapel to the left in 1774, where there is a canvas (*St. Filippo Neri in Ecstasy*) by Guercino, started in 1647 and completed with the addi-

vilizations, which has always characterized the ltural life of Bologna and its people, in the past in the present. This exhibit comprises about 0 pieces from some of the most prestigious collctions of Bologna, such as the Cospi and Pala- ones, whose items come from Italy and Eupe, Latin America, Africa and Asia.

In the nearby Neo-Gothic building, called *ıstellaccio* and built as a horse-shed after 1810, e can see the *Medieval and Renaissance lapiry* with important pieces, such as the *slab of e bambagina paper*, the *Renaissance Hebrew lae* and the controversial *inscription of Aelia lia Crispis* (this one a historical-literary curity). Nearby we can admire architectural and corative fragments dating back to the manesque period and the following ones, such the *Gothic mullioned window* from St. mes's or the big sandstone *Dalla Rovere coats arms*.

tion of the Virgin in 1662.

The sculptures are by Angelo Gabriello Piò (1690-1751).

In the second chapel, all the paintings are by Francesco Albani (1578-1660), the statues by Giovanni Tedeschi (1651).

The nice sacristy is really well preserved and also filled with quite valuable paintings, such as the *portrait of St. Filippo Neri* by Zuccari (1593).

The main chapel retains the big side angels made by Giuseppe Mazza (1653-1741) and the decoration designed by Francesco Galli from Bibiena (1653-1739).

By walking back along the right side of the church we come to a nice painting by Marcantonio Franceschini (1648-1729), *St. Francis of Sales with St. Francis of Assisi and St. Ann around the Virgin with Child in Glory.*

Another building by Architect Vignola is to be found in via Goito (3rd side street to the right of via dell'Indipendenza), **Palazzo Bocchi** (n. 16): in the basement there is an inscription in Latin verses by the poet Horace and a quotation in Hebrew from the Bible. The palace was built for Achille Bocchi who founded there in 1546 the Ermatena Academy. He commissioned the decorative works to Prospero Fontana who has left us, in a ground-floor room, the frescoes on the vault and an image of Hercules painted on a fire-place.

By walking through via Goito and turning right in via Albiroli, we come to the medieval **Guidozagni Tower**. If we turn left, instead, we come to via Marsala, in which we can still see houses dating back to the 13th century: **Palazzo Grassi** (n. 12), now the Officers' Club, still retains the beam arcade and the large ogee door; its chapel was painted in 1704 by Ercole Graziani.

By continuing our itinerary on via dell'Indipendenza, and in particular after the Cathedral, we can see the front of the **Monte di Pietà** (n. 11), in which the Canons of the Cathedral used to live and which was remodelled by architect Mario Bianchini in 1758. On the main door there is a round sculpture portraying a *Pietà on the dead Christ*; the inner courtyard with a two-tiered open gallery dates back to the end of the 15th century.

The **Palazzo dell'ex Seminario** (n. 8), which is now a section of the Baglioni Grand Hotel together with **Palazzo Fava**, stands right across from the Cathedral. The latter building still retains six magnificent rooms frescoed at the end of the 16th century. Three cycles of frescoes are attributed to the Carracci painters: the big hall, in which the *Adventures of Jason* are represented, the adjacent small room with the *Tales of Europa* and another one with the *Life of Aeneas, from the Trojan horse to his flight*, according to the episodes narrated in the 2nd and 3rd books of the Aeneid.

The **Teatro dell'Arena del Sole** (n. 44), designed in 1810 by Carlo Gasparri, clearly attests to the fact that, even before the project for the new layout of via dell'Indipendenza was

planned, this area of town was thought to be destined for the entertainment of the public through adequate structures. The front of the theatre, as well as the inside, was completely remodelled by Gaetano Rubbi in 1888; Alfredo Neri carved the statues for the façade.

The **Scalea della Montagnola** (the Montagnola steps), completed in 1896 according to the plan by Tito Azzolini and Attilio Muggia, is at the end of via dell'Indipendenza. It includes two really scenic flights of steps with a fountain by Diego Sarti at their base. The fountain is decorated with a sculpture, affectionately called by the people in Bologna the «Giant's wife», which instead represents a *horse and a naked woman attacked by a giant octopus*. By climbing the steps we come to the **Montagnola Park**. The hillock on which it stands was formed artificially to the north of the town's centre with the ruins of the Galliera Castle and in 1806 Architect Giovanni B. Martinetti arranged it as a garden and a public park with a symmetric layout of plants and trees. This area was set aside during the Napoleonic period for public use and entertainment. In fact, balloon flights, the game of greasy pole, race-horse meetings and a sort of bull hunt were all held there. The Montagnola park is mentioned by Stendhal in his book «Rome, Naples and Florence». **Piazza VIII Agosto** lies just in front of the Montagnola Park. Its name comes from the day in 1848 when the Austrian troops were defeated and chased from town but before the

was known as Market square because every Saturday in August a big livestock market had been held there at least since 1251. Now, every Friday and Saturday, a big market, known as **Piazzola**, is held in the square. This picturesque market is visited by different people, either looking for the latest fashion or for antique or simply second-hand things, that can be found browsing on the different stalls on either side of the street.

Santuario del Sacro Cuore (via Matteotti, 25). It was started in 1903, according to the design of Architect Edoardo Collamarini, for the Archbishop Domenico Svampa who had it built for the Order of St. Francis of Sales from the nearby Institute. When the church was finished in 1912, the archbishop had died five years before, and it was consecrated a year later by his successor, Monsignor Giacomo Della Chiesa, who became Cardinal the next year and two years later was elected Pope Benedict XV.

After the ruinous fall of the dome (1929), it was promptly restored. The church-shrine is decorated with the following paintings: *St. Giovanni Bosco* by Augusto Majani, 1937; the *Baptism of Christ*, the *Passage of St. Peter* and the *Saints Theresa and Rita* by Renato Pasqui, 1951; the *Holy Family* by Alessandro Franchi, 1905. The *Tomb of Cardinal Svampa* is in the crypt.

This church represents the highest example of 20th century religious architecture in Bologna; according to the style of that time, it combines Romanesque-Gothic elements with others inspired by Eastern art.

GALLERIA COMUNALE D'ARTE MODERNA

Outside porta Mascarella, within that modern area dominated by the white towers built by Architect Kenzo Tange, and near the fiera district, we can see the **Galleria comunale d'arte moderna** «Giorgio Morandi» (Municipal Modern Art Gallery), which was moved here in 1975 from Villa delle Rose (see pag. 192). The entrance to the Gallery is in piazza della Costituzione, 3 (tel. 502264-502859-503277). The Gallery, built according to the design by Leone Pancaldi, is connected to the *Palazzo della cultura e dei congressi*, planned in 1975 by Melchiorre Bega and Lieuwe Op'Land. The Gallery is divided into two floors and a basement of 2,000 square metres; each floor is provided with a central hall around which the exhibition areas rotate. The extraordinary wealth of 20th-century masterpieces (paintings, sculptures, drawings, etchings, etc.,

in all about 2,000 pieces) in the Municipal Gallery should form in turns its *permanent exhibition* but this has not proven very easy because up to now the Gallery has been mainly used for temporary art shows of excellent level. The collections in the gallery, acquired through bequests, donations and acquisitions, present artworks from the most important contemporary artists, from Bologna, Italy and abroad: Flavio and Luigi Bertelli, Nino Bertocchi, Umberto Boccioni, Remo Brindisi, Alberto Burri, Carlo Carrà, Athos Casarini, Felice Casorati, Carlo Corsi, Adolfo De Carolis, Giorgio De Chirico, Filippo De Pisis, Marx Ernst, Virgilio Guidi, Jean Ipousteguy, Carlo Leoni, Norma Mascellani, Sebastian Matta, Luciano Minguzzi, Jackson Pollock, Concetto Pozzati, Alfredo Protti, Bruno Saetti, Pio Semeghini, Ardengo Soffici, Mario Sironi, Graham Sutherland and many other famous artists.

Montagnola: the scenic stairway (1896). 2. The so-called «turtles'» basin. 3. Municipal Modern Art Gallery: the entrance.

MUSEO-LABORATORIO
MACCHINE SCUOLA INDUSTRIA

The Machinery-School-Industry-Laboratory-Museum is located in the technical secondary school, Istituto tecnico industriale Aldini-Valeriani, in via Sario Bassanelli 9, outside porta Galliera (tel. 358275-367930). It exhibits scientific teaching aids used in the school, permanently placed here after a show held there in 1980. The items exhibited date from over two centuries. The Institute, established in 1877-78 from the various changes of the *technical schools Aldini-Valeriani in Bologna*, opened in 1842-44 thanks to the bequests of Luigi Valeriani (1828) and Giovanni Aldini (1834), used also instruments from the 18th century. We can see equipment — and models — for physics experiments, equipment for biology and chemistry research, work tools built from 1750 to 1950 in Italy and Europe. Let us recall, among the many interesting items, the following: the models of Sebastiano Zavaglia from Bologna (1824-1876), of his helpers Antonio and Clodoveo Franchini, the ones built by the Mechanics Workshops of Castel Maggiore and other from abroad (such as Clair in Paris

and Breguet in Bern), and the outstanding En glish production.

The Museum can be visited on Mondays, Tuesdays Thursdays and Fridays from 9 a.m. to 1 p.m.; on Wed nesdays and Saturdays from 9 a.m. to 6 p.m. It i closed on holidays.

Closer to Porta Galliera, in via Vittorio Bigar 1, a *Museum of Public Transportation* for botl rail and road vehicles has been planned for some time, documenting mainly the Bologna area from the omnibus to the horse-draw tram through the present day.

---

1. Gallery of Modern Art. Renato Guttuso: the burial o Togliatti. 2. Monte Bibele: Etruscan-Gallic masonry.

A tour outside the town's gates

Outside PORTA MAGGIORE, by following ia Emilia Levante, we come to the spot called 'icogna, just after S. Lazzaro di Savena, where e can admire the 16th-century **Villa Cicogna** (ns. 42-244), built in 1570. An arcaded open gallery aarks both fronts; the running gallery inside is ecorated by tempera paintings, one of which illustrates how this villa should have appeared, had ne original plan, attributed to Vignola, been followed.

Also beyond San Lazzaro di Savena (the important **Archeological Museum «Luigi Donini»** to be found there in via Fratelli Canova 51, l. 465132, with items from prehistoric to Roman times found in the surrounding areas) the oad going through the Idice valley comes to Ionterenzio.

IONTERENZIO

Around 1970, in the area Pianella di Monte avino, at the eastern reaches of the Bibele Iountain, remains of a human settlements were found at 525 metres above sea level. Extensive excavation seasons from 1972 onwards have rought to light an **Etruscan-Celtic Village** from ne 4th-2nd centuries B.C. on artificial terrass-

ing, divided into *insulae*, with remains of dry walls with pebbles and sandstone slabs, a large *tank* for water supplies, and several elements suggesting the worship of deities related to agriculture. On the nearby peak of Monte Tamburino, excavations carried out in 1979 have brought to light a large *necropolis*: more than one hundred tombs have been found, one of which, probably of an official, has offered rich furnishings, including dishes and weapons. In the centre of Monterenzio, the **Museum of Monterenzio and of the Idice Valley «Luigi Fantini»**, opened in 1983, displays, in a rational and effective way and with clear captions, the items from the excavation season at Monte Bibele and Monte Tamburino: earthenware in terracotta, spindles and reels, hand-loom's weights, work tools (hoes, sickles, dogirons), black-painted dishes (cups, plates, bowls, kantaros, skyphos, phiale, olpe, etc.), metallic objects (buckles, rings, knives), glass and coins; there are also prehistoric items from the Bronze and Iron Ages and from the Roman colonization.

The Monterenzio Museum, located in the Casa della Cultura, can be visited on weekdays from 9 a.m. to 1 p.m., on Saturdays and holidays from 9 a.m. to 1 p.m. and from 3 to 6 p.m. It is closed on Mondays.

Outside PORTA S. STEFANO, by following

1

via Murri, we reach **Villa Aldrovandi** (ns. 17-19) in via Toscana, now the seat of Municipal offices for the Savena district, which was built in the second half of the 18th century by Francesco Tadolini as a copy of the Venetian villas of Palladio, as can be seen from emicyclic bargeboards, springing out of the building's main body. In the inside, the most interesting part of the villa is certainly the charming small theatre with balconies marked by painted-cloth sills, where the stucco caryatids by Petronio Tadolini hide the supporting elements with their slender bodies and their hands forward as if ready to receive wreaths and festoons, which were really placed there during shows and celebrations.

HISTORICAL TOY SOLDIE MUSEUM

Villa Aldrovandi, called Mazzacorati, hosts th «*Mario Massaccesi» Historical Toy Soldi Museum* on the groundfloor, named after its cre ator and first director (Bologna 1920-1981 Opened in 1973 in the Zambeccari building in P azza Calderini, it was moved here in 1991. In rather small area thousands of prized collecto items are displayed in glass cases, rare exemple of military models, war-game equipment. Mo of the toy soldiers on display are unique piece but there are also some extraordinarily charm ing sets. Especially through the Massaccesi co lection we can travel through nearly two centu ries of Italian, German, Frech, English, Russ an, etc. production, from the paper set of th pontifical army (circa 1820) to our own time with flat types, *demi-ronde, ronde, ronde boss* and the materials used in various periods: pape tin lead, aluminum, stucco, paste, plastic, an rubber, etc. Among the oldest pieces are tho by Adam Schweitzer from 1820, by Ammo from fürth (1880-1910), by Pellerin d'Epin (1870), by Heyde, Lucotte, Mignot, Lineo Gebrüder Schneider (1903-1904), Antonini. Th pieces are organized bty the period the represent.

The Historical Toy Soldier Museum may b visited Saturdays from 3 to 6:30 p.m., Sunda and holidays from 9:30 a.m. to 12:30 p.m. (Vi la Aldrovandi guardian: tel. 6234703). For visi by school groups, contact the director, Robert Nannetti, tel. 419102.

Hill up to **Villa Guastavillani** (n. 16), planned by Ottaviano Mascherino in 1575. From the villa, we can still have a magnificent view of rolling hills descending towards the Savena and Idice valleys. Its entrance door, in fact, more than marking the estate limits seems to act as a sort of perspective telescope on which to see the everchanging colours of the surrounding countryside. The inside still retains a large mosaic hall with seashells and also many richly-decorated rooms.

Outside PORTA S. FELICE, in via Marco Emilio Lepido, the Zagnoni family had a palace built in the second half of the 18th century. It is known as **Villa Pallavicini** (n. 198) and it is built in Palladian style as we can see from its tympanum. Its rooms still retain many tempera paintings attributed to Vincenzo Martinelli and Petronio Fancelli.

The State road Porrettana goes through the RENO VALLEY connecting many important centres lying among beautiful and verdant sceneries (at Casalecchio di Reno, the **Reno Locks** from the 12th century; at Pontecchio, the **Mausoleum of Guglielmo Marconi** by Marcello Piacentini:

Outside PORTA CASTIGLIONE, by following via Degli Scalini we climb up the Barbiano

1. Museum of Monterenzio: iron helmet with cheekprotection and bronze ornaments. 2. crockery from tomb fornitures. 3. Soldier Museum: exhibition hall. 4. Erik di Pomerania (Capelli Coll.). 5. Sardinian standard-bearer of 1848 and casting mould.

e great inventor was buried there in 1941; in
ie Villa Grifone, above the Mausoleum, Mar-
oni carried out his first radiotelegraphy experi-
ents in 1895; at Panico, the Romanesque **Pieve
i S. Lorenzo di Panico** from the 12th-13th cen-
iries). The road finally leads to MAR-
ABOTTO.

IARZABOTTO

In the centre of this small town we can see the
ssary **Temple**, dedicated to the 1830 civilians
ho died in October 1944 at the hands of the
azi «SS» troops guided by Major Reder under
eneral Kesserling. Marzabotto is also quite
nown for the extensive remains of an Etruscan
wn from the 6th-4th centuries B.C., located on
river plateau called Pian di Misano and com-
only known as **Misa**, lying within the impor-

tant archeological site at the south end of Marzabotto. Misa, the only pre-Roman town in
Northern Italy with an orthogonal plan, is divided by four large streets which mark eight building areas, further marked by other side streets.
An *insula* without building is the *agorà* or *forum*
area. The houses' foundations were made of peb-
ble and mortar. The continuous excavation seasons, from the 19th century up to now, have
brought to light metal *foundries* and *kilns* for
bricks and earthenware, and a *necropolis* outside
the eastern *town's gate*. In the Norht-West direction, there is another *necropolis* in the villa Aria
park and an *acropolis* with remains of four places
of worship, altars (one with a central well called
mundus), remains of an acqueduct. The excavations were started in 1831 by the Counts Giuseppe
and Pompeo Aria; they were continued by
Giovanni Gozzadini and Edoardo Brizio. Now
that the area falls under State control, the works
are carried out by the Archeological department.
All the items brought to light during excavation
works are exhibited in the **National Archeological Museum «Pompeo Aria»**, in which a clear
idea is given about Etruscan towns and their re-

5

6

*Villa Aldrovandi by Francesco Tadolini (18th century). 2.
lla Pallavicini (18th century). 3. Pontecchio, Villa Griffone
ack front). 4. Mausoleum of Guglielmo Marconi (1941).
Marzabotto: remains of Misa, an Etruscan town (detail).
The eastern necropolis (detail).*

219

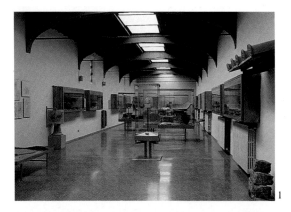

and earthenware, work tools and implemer furnishings, etc.

The archeological site is open everyday from 8 a to 7.30 p.m.; the Archeological Museum «Pom, Aria» can be visited everyday from 9 to 12 a.m. (from 3 to 6.30 p.m.; the Museum is closed on M days.

By continuing along via Porrettana, after small town of Vergato, after a few kilometres come to the **Mattei Rocchetta**, an amazing ed ce built in a plethora of styles on the ruins c Medieval fortress for Cesare Mattei in the secc half of the 19th century.

Nearby, on the left bank of the Reno river reach the Chiesa di Riola.

ligious and economic life. The museum comprises architectural fragments, objects with Etruscan inscriptions, tombs and burial furnishings, bronze, marble and terracotta statues, ceramics, dishes

CHIESA DI RIOLA

The first design for this church, dedicated t S. Maria Assunta, was made by architect Alva Aalto in 1966 on commission by the Card. Arch bishop Giacomo Lercaro, however, when th project was first shown to the public, it aros such strong controversies that the beginning o works was delayed for more than five years.

When finally the works began, under the direc tion of Vezio Nava, the collaborator of the Fir nish architect, and thanks also to the brillian operational solutions of Mario Tamburini, a nev design was used which envisaged the shortenin of the church by eliminating a span.

The works were completed by 1978 and th church amazed the onlooker right away, and sti does, for the architectural solution of Aalto, hi playing with the light, the inside use of space an materials so different from the traditional ones It is also impressive for its monumental size which is really enticing although quite far fron the traditional concept of a place of worship.

1. Pompeo Aria Archeological Museum: the new wing. 2 and 3. Pieces exhibited in the Museum. 4. Riola: the Mattei Rochetta (19th century). 5. Alvar Aalto's church completed in 1978: its very luminous inside. 6. Russian icon. 7. View of the church from the riverside Reno.

7

221

BOLOGNA

alma mater studiorum

Legenda:

1. Municipal Palace and Municipal Art Collections - Morandi Museum
2. Podestà Palace
3. Basilica of St. Petronius
4. Neptune's Fountain
5. King Enzo's Palace
6. The Two Towers
7. Merchants' Palace
8. Old Pepoli Palace
9. Margherita's Gardens and Church of S. Maria della Misericordia
10. Ruini-Ranuzzi Palace, today's Court Hall
11. Basilica and Shrine of St. Dominic
12. Historical Museum of Toy soldiers
13. Archiginnasio and the Civic Archeologic Museum
14. Church of S. Maria della Vita
15. Basilica of St. Stephen
16. Church of S. Giovanni in Monte
17. Church of S. Maria del Baraccano
18. Carducci Museum and Library Civic Risorgimento Museum
19. Basilica of St. Anthony of Padua
20. Basilica of Ss. Bartolomeo and Gaetano
21. Davia-Bargellini Palace - Civic Museum of Industrial Art and Davia Bargellini Gallery
22. Basilica of Santa Maria dei Servi
23. Fantuzzi Palace
24. Church of Ss. Vitale and Agricola
25. Malvezzi de Medici Palace
26. Conservatory of Music
27. Church of S. Giacomo Maggiore
28. Municipal Theatre
29. Poggi Palace and University's Museums
30. National Picture Gallery
31. Bentivoglio Palace
32. Basilica of St. Martin
33. Church of S. Giovanni Battista de Celestini
34. State Archives
35. Bevilacqua Palace

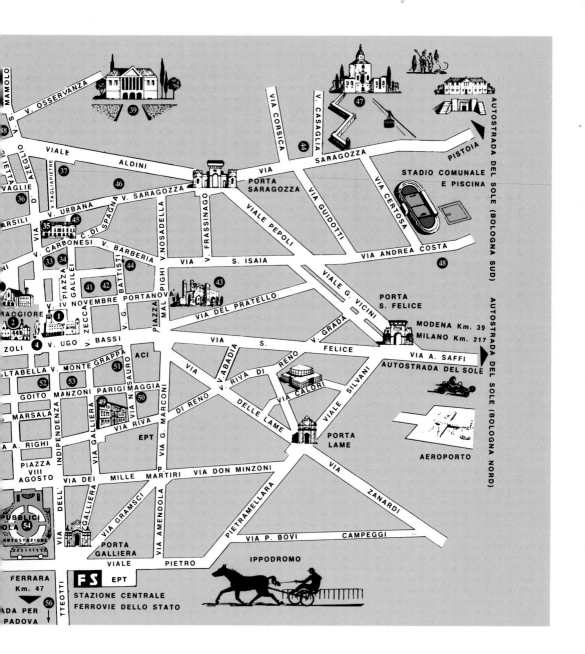

INDEX

LA FOTOMETALGRAFICA EMILIANA SRL
San Giovanni in Persiceto - Bologna

Printed in Italy